"If Any Man Would Follow Me ..."

"If Any Man Would Follow Me ..."

Lance Lambert

LANCE LAMBERT MINISTRIES

Richmond, Virginia, USA

Originally Published by:
Two-fish Publications
Corona, California
Copyright © 2012

ISBN: 978-1-68389-029-4

www.lancelambert.org

Contents

Introduction

If any man come after Me, let him deny himself, take up his cross, and follow Me. These words, spoken by the Lord Jesus without any preamble are the very heart of discipleship. Here we have the heart of what it is to be a child of God. This is not just something to do with deeper life, this lies at the center of the gospel.

Inherent within our very salvation, is a surrender to the authority of God. When He is dwelling in us, untrammeled by our will, when we have let go of that self-life, and when He is Lord, we find that He will overcome in us. The question is not how to live the Christian life but how to die. If we learn to die with Christ, the Christian life will take care of itself—blossoming, growing and bearing fruit.[1]

---

1 Messages spoken in various places: Christian Family Conference 7/2/81, Richmond, VA 11/8/03, Christian Family Conference 6/28/10, Christian Family Conference 6/29/10, and Christian Family Conference 6/30/10

1.
Living Faith and the Work of the Cross

The Heart of the Gospel

Colossians 2:20–3:5a

If ye died with Christ from the rudiments of the world, why, as though living in the world, do ye subject yourselves to ordinances, Handle not, nor taste, nor touch (all which things are to perish with the using), after the precepts and doctrines of men? Which things have indeed a show of wisdom in will-worship, and humility, and severity to the body; but are not of any value against the indulgence of the flesh.

If then ye were raised together with Christ, seek the things that are above, where Christ is, seated on the right hand of God. Set your mind on the things that are above, not on the things that are upon the earth. For ye died, and your life is hid with Christ in God. When Christ, who is our life, shall be manifested, then shall ye also with him be manifested in glory. Put to death therefore your members which are upon the earth.

Galatians 2:20

I have been crucified with Christ; and it is no longer I that live, but Christ liveth in me: and that life which I now live in the flesh I live in faith, the faith which is in the Son of God, who loved me, and gave himself up for me.

Romans 6:3–12a

Or are ye ignorant that all we who were baptized into Christ Jesus were baptized into his death? We were buried therefore with him through baptism into death: that like as Christ was raised from the dead through the glory of the Father, so we also might walk in newness of life. For if we have become united with him in the likeness of his death, we shall be also in the likeness of his resurrection; knowing this, that our old man was crucified with him, that the body of sin might be done away, that so we should no longer be in bondage to sin; for he that hath died is justified from sin. But if we died with Christ, we believe that we shall also live with him; knowing that Christ being raised from the dead dieth no more; death no more hath dominion over him. For the death that he died, he died unto sin once: but the life that he liveth, he liveth unto God. Even so reckon ye also yourselves to be dead unto sin, but alive unto God in Christ Jesus. Let not sin therefore reign in your mortal body.

Let us have a word of prayer:

Dear Lord, we have already stood by faith under that anointing which is ours in the Lord Jesus, and all we want to do now is to ask Thee that

Thou wilt cause Thy word to live to us. And Lord, we pray that the burden for this time may somehow be communicated clearly by the Holy Spirit. Oh grant, Lord, that this Word of Christ may come to dwell in us richly. Make it like that we pray in the name of our Lord Jesus. Amen.

Possessing What is Rightfully Ours in Christ

There is a great need in these days in which we live for the Lord's people to have a living, practical, working faith. This is not a faith which is just to do with a mental ascent to Christian doctrine or to the authority and inspiration of the Bible, but the kind of faith which unites us to the Word of God. This means that the Word of Christ comes to dwell in us richly and we receive the implanted Word. It begins to take root in us, then grows up and bears fruit. We need that kind of faith which means that all we find in this Book can become our experience as we move on with the Lord. I say "can be"; I would like to say *all* that is in the Book *should* become our experience, but can anyone in one single life enter into all that is in this Book? It will surely take eternity to experience all that is ours in the Lord Jesus. However, if we were only possessing a fraction of what is ours in Him compared to what we have in the future, that would be very good; but most of us are not. We are right on the edge in the shallows, right on the perimeter of things. We are saved by the grace of God, knowing forgiveness of sin, but have not gone very far beyond that. That is why we need to consider this matter of living faith—possessing what is ours in the Lord Jesus.

God has given to us the fullness and the power of the Holy Spirit—both the indwelling and the empowering of the Holy Spirit. It is ours—not because you and I are worthy, nor because you and I are zealous or pray enough; it is because of the finished work of the Messiah. That complete and finished work of the Lord Jesus and all the work of the Holy Spirit belong to every child of God. Now it does not mean we enter into everything all at once, but thank God it is all ours. Thus, the moment we see it with the eyes of our heart we can put our feet down, as it were, and claim what is ours in Him and move in to possess it.

The Work of the Cross

Jesus Died For Us

Let us consider this matter of living faith and the work of the cross. The work of the cross has two sides to it. Christ died *for* us and Christ died *as* us. Christ died as my substitute; that is, He substituted Himself in my place and did what I could not do. Being without sin, He bore in His own body my sin; God made Him to become my sin that I might become the righteousness of God in Him (see II Corinthians 5:21). Is that not amazing? That is the work of the cross. That is when the Lord Jesus died as my atonement, when He died as my substitute, in my place. I could not do that; I cannot go there; only He could do that work. Now I think most of us, if only dimly, do understand that part of the work of the cross. We know that we cannot be saved but by the Lamb of God. We know that He, who is our Passover Lamb, is the only way by which we can come to God, the only way that we can be born of God, the only way we can be redeemed and saved.

Jesus Died As Our Representative

However, He not only died as my substitute, He died as my representative. That is, when He died on the cross, He represented you and me. When He was crucified, you and I were crucified; when He was buried, you and I were buried; when God raised Him from the dead, you and I were raised from the dead to walk in newness of life; and when He was seated at the right hand of God the Father, you and I were seated together with Him in heavenly places. Now what a marvelous thing this is! So tremendous is this whole matter that the apostle Paul said by inspiration of the Holy Spirit: "For ye died, and your life is hid with Christ in God. When Christ, who is our life, shall appear, you also shall be manifested together with Him in glory" (see Colossians 3:3–4). He died as our representative; that is, He died as me.

Only By Revelation Can We See

This Work that Christ Has Done

Now you may not yet fully understand this. I know that for years I had no idea about this side of the cross and wandered in a morass of Christian works doing my very best to be a good Christian, to witness, to pray, to read my Bible, to look holy, as well as to be holy, to be everything possible. I did every single thing that was possible in order to be a Christian because I was entirely ignorant of this thing. I read the Bible, but it is so amazing how you can read things and they just do not mean anything to you. Although I had read the Bible I did not really know anything about the Holy Spirit. It came as a great shock to me when I discovered that the Holy Spirit is within me and can come upon me. I had read John's gospel numerous times and had read those words in which Jesus said: "I will give you another Comforter and He shall be with you forever" (see John 14:16), but it never entered my heart. I had read about the Spirit of truth leading us into all truth, about the Spirit taking the things of Christ, and declaring them to us, and yet it was just as if there was no Holy Spirit until the day that God opened the eyes of my heart. Suddenly I saw that the Holy Spirit was come and that He had taken up residence within me. When I had drunk of that living water and had received the Lord Jesus, the Holy Spirit had come within, and then I understood that He could not only be within but also upon one. Oh! Then it seemed to me that every other paragraph in the Word of God somehow related to the Holy Spirit. Everywhere I read I saw: "The Spirit this, the Spirit that, the Spirit the other."

It is the same when you have seen this work of the cross and what God has done with you and with me. It is amazing. We can read, "I have been crucified with Christ, nevertheless, I live, yet not I ...," and it does not mean anything to us; it just goes through one ear and out of the other. It just flitters across the eyes; that is all. We can read: "The world is crucified unto me and I to the world," and it just goes over our head; it does not mean anything. We read that we are to deny ourselves, take up our cross and follow Him, and it goes in this ear and out of the other; it has no meaning. It is as if it is not there. We read it, yet it has no meaning until the eyes of our heart are illuminated and the Spirit of wisdom and revelation is given to us. Then it is as if our eyes open and we see something—we *see* what God has done with us.

Now it is a marvelous thing to have our sins dealt with. Can anyone be saved unless they know, however dimly, that Jesus bore away our sins? Having had our sins borne away and canceled out we are justified before God; that is, in the sight of God it is just as if we had never sinned. We are given the divine and spotless record of the Lord Jesus as our own. God substitutes His sinless history for mine and says, "From now on this is your history. It is just as if you had never sinned." Is that not marvelous? Our sins have been canceled out, blotted out, cast away as far as the east is from the west, blotted out as a thick cloud, never to be remembered again. When God deals with sin, He never again raises it up. It is done, it is finished. It was Luther who once had a dream and came to God to ask about certain sins, and God said, "What sins?" And Luther said, "You must surely remember." And God said, "I see no sins," and He drew Martin Luther's eyes to a table where there was a book and he saw written on it: "Martin Luther." When he opened the book, in it was written *"perfect righteousness,"* and when Martin Luther questioned it, God said, "I do not know of any sin."

Sin Has Been Borne Away but the Self-Life Remains

Jesus has borne away all our sin and in the place of our sinful, depraved, dark record, we have the record of the spotless, sinless Son of God. Now that is the most marvelous and wonderful thing; but having said that we come to a practical problem. You cannot be a Christian for very long before you discover that even if you know your sins have been dealt with, you still have a big problem, and it is your *self.* Sometimes we think that if we were only noble, beautiful, and sweet people we would have no problem; but we would still have a huge problem.

Most of us are very egocentric. We like to be taken note of; we have rights. Even without sin, we have rights. We do not want people treading over our rights, we do not want to be treated like a doormat, we do not want someone tarnishing our reputation, we do not want someone striking us; we will strike them back! If they take our coat we will grab it back and take theirs! We may be noble and beautiful but we have rights. Rights! Just because we have no sin problem, it does not mean we have no rights. We have rights, and this is the whole problem with human beings—*I*. Sin is the problem—s-I-n—"I" in the center. It is so simple.

God has answered this whole problem. He has not only dealt with sins, He has dealt with sin. He has not only dealt with the things we do—our evil works, all our mistakes and breakdown, all that is an abomination in His sight—but He deals with the self-life that lies at the heart of the whole problem.

The Impossibility of Crucifying One's Self

Now let me just say a few things about this whole matter of being crucified with Christ. First of all I would like to underline the impossibility of crucifying one's self. In Christian circles, if there is any understanding of this, sometimes all it amounts to is a headache. Someone says, "I have my cross back again," they mean they have a headache or a twinge in the hip, or their affliction, whatever it is. Some people look upon that as the cross they have to bear. That is *not* what the Lord Jesus meant at all.

When people have seen a little of the meaning of our Lord Jesus' words on denying self and taking up their cross and following Him, they start on the road of trying somehow or other to crucify themselves. It is an impossible job. Now if you think for a few moments of the very picture of crucifixion, of course it is impossible. You can possibly nail a nail through one hand, and you might even be able to get down and nail one through your feet, but what do you do with the other hand? It is impossible to crucify one's self. It is quite obvious, and yet Christians go round trying to put themselves to death, trying to fall into the ground and die, trying to put to death the deeds or the works of the flesh; it is an impossible job. No wonder Christians are so miserable! When once this thing dawns on you and you begin to understand there is a way of the cross to walk, Christians who sometimes see it become the most miserable, the most somber, the most dark, and the most heavy of all Christians. This is because somehow or other we try to crucify ourselves. We try to die, but we cannot do it. It is a quite false concept.

The trouble is that every time you push down one part of self, it comes up in another place. I always think of one of those old-fashioned air cushions. If you pushed one side down it came up on the other side, and if you pushed the other side down it came up on the opposite side. The air is in the air cushion and it must come up somewhere. So anywhere you pushed it down, it would come back up. And some Christians spend their whole time suppressing something, and then suddenly they discover that something else is coming up and they suppress that. Then it is back again where they started, and they try to suppress both things and then it is somewhere else! It is an impossible business. No wonder of all people we feel the most miserable. It is bound to be like that. The Lord did say it would be a difficult job living the Christian life and that we would have many tribulations entering into the Kingdom of God; but do you really think that He has given us such an impossible task that we are sort of wrestling all the time with this thing?

The Dock Weed

It is like this weed we call in Britain "Dock weed." Most people who are not good gardeners, when they see the Dock weed growing, rush out and snatch it from the ground and it looks good—for two days. Then it is broken up and it scatters. Then they think, "All right, we will try another method." And they shovel and shovel, but every little piece that is left in the ground becomes another Dock weed.

And that is just the same with this old nature of ours. We go to town and have a blitzkrieg on it. "I have just heard a marvelous message on walking the way of the cross, so now I have got to do it. I have got to get hold of myself and do this work." And so we blitz the whole thing and break it up and say, "Oh! This is marvelous. I feel so good about it, you know. I have given myself a real hit, and I believe I have done it. I have crucified myself at last!" Only later we find that in place of one Dock weed we have twelve. Then we have another blitz bigger than the one before with more prayer and even perhaps a little bit of fasting, and we blitz the whole thing only to discover after a few days that we now have 24 or 30 plants in place. And in the end we give up and think, "I must be the black sheep. All these people are singing about victory and chains falling off and joy in the Lord—and here I am."

I was in an assembly of Christians for some years where we used to sing those wonderful Wesley hymns such as, "And can it be that I should gain an interest in the Saviour's blood?" In that hymn there is a stanza:

"Long my imprisoned spirit lay,
Fast bound in sin and nature's night,
Thine eye diffused a quickening ray,
I woke, the dungeon flamed with light;
My chains fell off, my heart was free,
I rose went forth and followed Thee."

I used to look at all those shining faces, sing and think to myself, "I know I am saved but those chains have not fallen off me." I did not dare tell anyone because I thought I was the black sheep of the flock. Years later I discovered that most of them were singing it in faith!

I remember years ago hearing Bob Mumford say on this matter of being crucified with Christ that he had an experience and thought that he had finally died with Christ, only to discover a little later that he had only fainted! But is that not the experience of all of us when it really comes down to it? When we do not really see this matter and we hear a marvelous message about it, we take hold of it in some way. We try to stir up everything that is in us and pump up faith. Finally, we grasp the truth; and for a moment it seems, "I am dead with Christ!" And perhaps we can smile at someone who is insulting us for 24 hours or perhaps 48 hours or even a few days. Then suddenly it is too much of a strain, and we are back again where we were. It is impossible to crucify one's self, and yet this matter is essential. It lies at the very heart of the gospel.

The Watering Down of the Gospel

What a sad and tragic thing it has been, this watering down of the gospel we preach. In Mark's Gospel he said this: "And He called unto Him the multitude with his disciples, and said unto them, If any man would come after me, let him deny himself, and take up his cross, and follow me. For whosoever would save his life shall lose it; and whosoever shall lose his life for my sake and the gospel's shall save it. For what doth it profit a man, to gain the whole world, and forfeit his life? For what should a man give in exchange for his soul?" (8:34–35) Now this is interesting to me. First of all, it was to the whole multitude with the disciples, secondly we take the last part of that as pure gospel message: "What shall it profit a man if he gain the whole world and lose his own soul or what will a man give in exchange for his soul." But this verse is evidently something to do with deeper teaching. The Lord Jesus put this whole matter right at the heart of the gospel.

And the apostle Paul, by the Spirit of God, brings the two together: "I have been crucified with Christ, nevertheless, I live, yet not I but Christ liveth in me and the life which I now live, I live by the faith of the Son of God who loved me and gave himself up for me" (Galatians 2:20). That is what we often call the simple gospel: He loved me and gave himself up for me, and the deeper life teaching is: I have been crucified with Christ.

One of the most terrible things that has come into Christian circles in the last hundred years is this cheapening of the gospel. Now I do not for a single moment want to say anything against people like D. L. Moody, Reuben Torrey or Billy Graham who I believe were anointed servants of God. However, when we look at so much of the cheap imitation of their preaching, what have we got? We have a kind of *decision* preaching. It is like an American presidential election: "Who will you vote for, President Jesus or President Satan? Who will you cast your vote for?" And then the challenge comes to decide. No wonder people know nothing about the Lordship of Jesus Christ; no wonder people know nothing about surrendering to the Lord Jesus; no wonder they have such a battle about obeying God. They believe: "If I choose someone, I am an equal." In a way it is psychological. No one who preaches this means it, but it is a devalued gospel because by simple decision preaching human beings have put themselves into a position where they feel they are something. We are voting for someone or we are deciding for someone; therefore, they should be very pleased about it. We are going to vote for them and choose them.

A Command to Obedience

I do not find this in the New Testament. I find in the New Testament a command to obey the gospel. Now when there is a command to obedience, immediately the whole psychological atmosphere is different. It means that in order to obey, the whole question of authority has come in.

A young fellow came to me just a few weeks ago in a house gathering that I was leading. I had no idea that he did not know the Lord Jesus, that he was not saved. I had noticed him and his dear wife and their four beautiful children. I was very interested in the family because I had never seen a family with two sets of twins, and it attracted me to them. And then one day he came up to me and said, "Oh, I have such a problem."

And I said, "What is your problem?" I was fully expecting that he was going to pour out some problem to do with being a believer.

He said, "I just do not know what to do? I believe in the living God, but I just cannot believe in the Lord Jesus as you call Him. What should I do? I feel it is hopeless."

"I do not think it is hopeless at all. You believe in the living God?"

So he said, "Yes I do."

And I replied: "Very well." Now this is not exactly Biblical but it is how the Lord led me at that point. I said, "You do believe in the living God?"

"Yes, I do."

"Then," I said, "you must obey Him."

"Oh," he said, "and what does He want?"

"You must obey Him—you must repent and believe on the Lord Jesus."

He thought for a moment and then said, "How do I do that?"

And I said, "Very simply."

He began to weep, and before long he passed from death unto life. It was a matter of obedience. He could not make the choice because he had a problem. But when it came to him by the Spirit that he must obey God and take the leap of faith, God saved him.

And when I left him he was in no doubt about the Person of the Lord Jesus. After a few days he was reveling in the Lord Jesus and worshipping Him.

Oh, what we have done to this gospel that has been given to us. Everywhere in the book of Acts the apostles commanded people to believe on the Lord Jesus. They commanded repentance and faith. And that brings the whole question of the authority of God and of His Christ into view and the fact that inherent within our becoming disciples, becoming believers, within our very salvation, is a surrender to the authority of God. We have to obey.

Giving Up All Rights to Ourselves

It is interesting to me that the Lord Jesus put it like this. He did not say, "Now listen everybody, you are going to have to make a choice between Me or the prince of this world, between darkness or light. And once you have made that choice you must understand that if you would come after Me, later on, perhaps some years, you must deny yourself, take up your cross, and follow Me." No; the Lord Jesus, without any preamble, said: "If any man come after Me, let him deny himself, take up his cross, and follow Me!" Here we have the very heart of discipleship. Here we have the very heart of what it is to be a child of God. We are to give up, as one modern version puts it, all rights to ourselves, take up our cross and follow Him.

Now anyone who takes up his cross has no more rights. He has just some hours or so to live, which is the time between when he is sentenced and when he is to be executed. That is all; he has no further rights. There is no question of expediency or of compromising because there are no more rights. He has given up all rights. His life is over; he is finished. When Jesus said this, it was stark: "If any man come after Me, let him give up all right to himself, take up his cross and follow Me. He that saveth his life, that is, he that seeks to preserve his life, shall lose it! And he that loses his life for My sake and the gospel's, the same shall find it."

Uncrucified Self-Life Hinders Fullness of Life and Power

Now I personally do not believe that this is all in the future. I have no doubt that there is much in the future. Those that lose their lives now will surely find a fullness of life, a reward, a position in the kingdom which will be so much greater than any loss they suffer. However, it seems to me in my little life and ministry, that wherever I have discovered people who are full of joy, sometimes full of laughter, full of life that is overflowing, those rivers going out, and who are clothed with power from on high, I have discovered people who have lost their lives. In losing their lives, they have already found life eternal. They not only have the right to life eternal as something in the future, but they are enjoying life eternal now. The problem is that it is not just sins that stop us from coming into the fullness of life and of power; it is sin which is your uncrucified self. Even if it is noble and beautiful and aristocratic and all the rest of it, it will still effectively stop you from coming into the fullness of life and power. It has to be removed. How is it to be removed?

Likewise I notice those Christians who, as they get older, become darker and darker and narrower and narrower, and smaller and pettier, and mean. There is no more life in them, and you have to by faith find Christ crucified in them. I have discovered that they are people who have clung to their lives; they have not lost their life for His sake and the gospel's. And when we seek to preserve our lives, we discover that we have lost them.

You may be fighting this battle of self-preservation—you are frightened the Lord might want you to be single, He might want you to marry, He may want you to go to some dreadful place on the other side of the earth, He may be requiring you to enter into and commit yourself to a company of believers, but you are afraid of the discipline and what it will cost. It is all self-preservation. Of course, you are glossing it all up in lovely spiritual terms and saying things like this: "I do not believe God wants me to be miserable like that, I do not believe that God would not give me that. I do not like conferences very much, particularly some that tell me I have to lose my life. I do not believe God is like that." We gloss it up in spiritual words, but it is self-preservation. It is the spontaneous, automatic fight of your self-life to preserve itself intact, to preserve its identity, to preserve your control over its destiny. You do not want to let it go. But there can be no Christian life, no Christian service, and no church life until you have let go of your life for His sake and the gospel's. You can be in the midst of a group that knows something about the body of Christ and others may be functioning, but you will be a spectator because you are fighting this battle of self-preservation.

God Saved Us to Be Overcomers

I know so many people who have the truth in their mind, but they are always on the perimeter. They never commit themselves. They are the critics, always standing on the outside looking in and saying, "Well, I do not like this, but I think this is good; I do not think that was so good." But they never commit themselves. It is the battle for the preservation of one's self.

This is not just something to do with deeper life; this lies at the heart of the gospel. The Lord Jesus did not want to save people who were living contradictions forever after. He has saved you and you are supposed to have peace which passes understanding; yet you have restlessness and you are neurotic. God has saved you and instead of having joy unspeakable and being filled with glory in a time of affliction, you are miserable. God has saved you that you might overcome; instead, you are totally defeated. God has saved you that you might be a son of light, but you are living in the darkness, fearful and afraid. God has saved you that you might know perfect love and all you know is the bondage of fear which has torment.

Does the Lord Jesus want to save people so that they might become living contradictions to Himself, to His salvation and to His gospel? No; He said, "When the Holy Spirit is come upon you, you shall be witnesses unto Me" (see Acts 1:8). He wants people who are free, who have peace which passes understanding even in the inexplicable, who have joy unspeakable and full of glory, who know that the kingdom of God is not eating and drinking, but righteousness, peace and joy in the Holy Spirit; people who know how it is to live a life of fullness. That is why He said, "If any man would come after me, let him give up all right to himself, take up his cross, and follow Me."

Men Want Christ Without the Cross

Have you followed very far if you have not found the cross in your path? What kind of Christian life have you been living? What kind of church life are you involved in if it escapes the cross? Samuel Rutherford once said: "Men want Christ cheap; they want Him without the cross, but the price will not come down." Do you want Christ without the cross? That is, you want the salvation, the joy, the peace, the fullness, and the power, but you do not want the cross. Then you will know that joy, peace, fullness and power for just a few weeks of your Christian life—and that is all. Once that self-centered principle takes over again: "give me, give me, give me; I want, I want, I want; what am I getting?"—then you will discover before very long that you become of all people the most miserable, the most empty, the most dark, the most unhappy, and the most restless because you are a living contradiction to the gospel. The gospel has no neutral ground.

Frances Ridley Havergal once ended one of her great hymns—"Like A River Glorious" with these words: "They who trust Him wholly find Him wholly true." Oh, the joy, the peace, the fullness, and the power that has been provided for us in the Promised Land. But there is no way to go over into that land except through Jordan, and Jordan is a picture of the cross. It is a picture of being crucified with Christ. You will recall that they took 12 stones and put them in the center of the river bed, and they took another 12 stones and put them on the bank of the Promised Land so that when the waters came back, the 12 stones in the river bed were covered forever. It was a picture of the cross. We are crucified with Christ, buried with Christ, and raised to walk in newness of life with Christ. There is no other way into this Promised Land. We cannot get our inheritance by hanging on to our self-life and keeping it intact.

Maybe you think that only the bad and base qualities in your self-life need to be dealt with, that there are a lot of nice, noble sweet qualities in you which just need to be polished up. However, God says, "No, good and bad, I am finished with you. I want to recreate you in My Son."

The New Creation in Christ

What a wonderful word that is in II Corinthians 5: "If any man be in Christ, he is a new creature: the old things are passed away; behold, they are become new. But all things are of God" (vv. 17–18a). I do not really like that rendering *new creature* because it leads us to a wrong idea of always looking inside for the new creature. We begin to say: "Where is he? If we are a new creature and old things are passed away, and all things are of God, where is this new man or this new creature?" I like the rendering that puts it like this which is perfectly faithful to the Greek: "Wherefore if any man be in Christ, *there* is a new creation." Oh, thank God, the new creation is not in my old man, but it is in Christ. This will deliver you from all kinds of accusations and condemnation of trying to know where this new creature is. Where are the old things that have passed away? And where are the things that have become new and are of God? They are all in

Christ. In the land there were 12 new stones, representing every one of the 12 tribes, erected on the bank of the river Jordan in the Promised Land.

There is No Resurrection Without Crucifixion

You may say to me: "All right, we have to take up our cross; we have got to give up all right to ourselves. But how do we do it? How do we lose our life?" The deepest instinct in any man or woman is self-preservation. We could prove this by throwing a person who cannot swim into a pool. They would fight like fury even if someone came to save them and would nearly drown that person as well. This instinct of self-preservation is the strongest instinct in a human being. How then can anyone lose their own life for His sake? We know we *ought* to, we may even have got to the place where we know we *have* to, but *how* to do it? Is that not the problem? Then we start on the wearisome business of trying to crucify ourselves or trying to put to death the deeds of the body. What an impossible job it really is! Jesus said: "Take up *his* cross." We are so thankful that He did not say: "If any man would come after Me, let him deny himself, and take up *My* cross." It was the Lord's cross, but He said take up *his* cross, as if the Lord's cross must be your cross.

This principle of the cross is one of the most tremendous things in the whole Bible. What is this principle? There can be no life without death. There can be no exaltation without humbling. There can be no wholeness without brokenness. There can be no summer without winter. There can be no harvest without a falling into the ground and dying on the part of seed. There can be no fruit without pruning. You cannot know resurrection without crucifixion. So if you want to know the fullness of that life and the power of His resurrection, it is in direct measure to what you know of being crucified together with Him. I pray that God may reveal this to every one of us, not as something heavy and dark but as the way into power, into life, and into fullness.

The Sign of the Dove Upon the Lord Jesus

The Lord Jesus went down into the waters of the Jordan to be baptized, and the Holy Spirit came down upon Him like a dove. People have interpreted this important event in various ways such as: "It was the anointing upon the Lord Jesus." Or, "The dove is the symbol of harmlessness, purity, and gentleness." But it does not satisfy me. Although we know the Lord Jesus was harmless, separate from sinners, undefiled, I do not feel that was the symbolism of the Holy Spirit coming upon Him like a dove. For me it is explained in this way. If you were a wealthy Jew you brought a heifer to be sacrificed for your sins. If you were middle-class you brought a ram or a lamb, but if you belonged to the vast multitude of the poor, you brought two turtledoves. And when John the Baptist saw the Holy Spirit coming down on the Lord Jesus like a dove, he immediately understood the significance of it and said: *Behold, the Lamb of God, that beareth away the sin of the world* (John 1:29b). In other words, he saw the Holy Spirit coming upon this One to enable Him to die. The Lord Jesus was committing Himself to the cross in the waters of the river Jordan three years before He died. He did not need to be baptized because He had no sin to confess or to be repented of. He went down into those waters because they were a picture of death, and He was baptized into that death three years before He came to Calvary. He died daily through all the three and a half years of His ministry. And it was the Holy Spirit who came upon Him to enable Him to do just that and, finally, to offer Himself up to God without spot or blemish on the cross.

In this matter of the cross what has God done with you and me? In His infinite mercy and wisdom, not only did God give the Lord Jesus as the one who *died in our place* but gave the Lord Jesus as the one who died *as* us. And when He died on the cross, it was as though God saw every one of us *in Christ*. When Christ was crucified, we were crucified. Paul did not say, as it is recorded in the King James Version: *I am crucified with Christ.* He said: *I "have been" crucified with Christ.* Our old man was crucified with Christ. It happened when Christ died in the amazing wisdom of God.

Liberated to Walk in Newness of Life

Once we begin to see it like that I think it changes our whole concept. The day I saw this truth it came like a bomb, as if I was hit between the eyes. Of course, I saw first this whole matter of the Holy Spirit, and I must tell you straightaway, I do not believe it is possible to know the work of the cross apart from the Holy Spirit. If we try to come to the work of the cross apart from the Holy Spirit, it is a work of the flesh. It is religion; it is will-worship, severity to the body, will-humility, a false humility, an artificial humility. It is not the real thing. We can afflict our bodies, we can try to look drab and dreary, we can try to be crucified; we can do it all, but what does it amount to? Nothing!

Do you think God is interested in pulverizing you? Did God save you so He could squash you into the ground, obliterate you, and cut you into little pieces? People have this strange idea about God, and it is no wonder they are frightened of Him and have a wrong kind of fear of Him. It is not that loving, wonderful respect for the Lord, but a terrible fear of God as if He is some terrible school master or terrible tyrant who wants to grind them into the ground, who wants to kill them or destroy them. That is not the meaning of the cross. The whole thought of the cross is that by bringing this self-life of ours—which has the poison of the serpent in it—to an end by the cross, you might be liberated to walk in newness of life and know what it is to sit with Christ in heavenly places. That is why God wants you to come this way. God knows that the only way you can come into life eternal, into the fullness of that life now, is by losing your life for His sake and the gospel's.

God Put Us in Christ

I have no better way of describing this than the way Elizabeth Fischbacher described it to me from brother Nee years ago. It is not my illustration. She said, "This piece of paper is you and this Bible is Christ, and just as I am putting this paper in this Bible, God took you and put you in Christ. Thus, you can no longer see the paper; you can only see the Bible." So it is with you. God put you in Christ and whatever happens to Him happens to you. If I put the Bible on the table, the piece of paper is on the table.

If I take the Bible up and put it into my hand, the paper is here in my hand. You cannot see it but it is there because it is in the Bible. Wherever I put the Bible or carry it, the paper is there because it is in the Bible. The history of the Bible has become the history of the piece of paper which is in it.

God, who lives in the ever present, took you, although you live thousands of years after the event, and put you into His Son; when He crucified His Son, He crucified you. When His Son was buried, you were buried out of sight; and when He raised His Son, you were raised to walk in newness of life. When His Son sat down, you sat down together with Him in heavenly places in Christ Jesus. Now I know that you can hear all this and it can just tickle your minds, but when it shines into the heart, you want to burst out of your skin!

God Crucified the Old Man

When I saw it for the first time with the eyes of my heart, it was as if the gospel was being preached to me for the first time. I could not believe it! I had spent four or five years beating Lance Lambert, pushing Lance Lambert, dressing him up in Christian clothes, forcing Christian phraseology into his mouth, forcing him onto his knees to pray, kicking him and beating him to make him a good zealous Christian, making him witness every day to someone about their soul's salvation until the people were frightened to death of me. And what was I after five years? The most miserable person you could ever wish to meet! However, I know that I got released from that miserable state on the day

I saw God had crucified me with Christ. I was so thrilled that all the artificiality, all the facade, all the projection of spirituality which was not real, which did not come out of real life and was like a kind of false theatrical thing, could go because God was not bothered about that old man. He was not trying to dress up the old man or Christianize him or make him sweet; He crucified the old man! And when I saw that I said, "Oh, my dear Lord, I have had the shoe on the wrong foot. I have been trying my best to Christianize that old man; and what have You done with him? You have crucified him. I have been trying to resurrect him, and You have finished with him. I was trying to get the good things from him—which I felt were quite a few—and the bad things I was trampling under foot. The trouble was that the bad things grew by the day as I held on to the good things. However, God said: "I crucified the lot." And that was a terrible shock! It was like a great burden or heavy weight on my back had just rolled away.

It Takes Living Faith to Lose Your Life

You have to see it with the eye of faith. What is living faith? No person can ever come to the place in their mind where they are willing to lose their life unless they have living faith. We feel it is better to hang on to the old self-life we have than to let it go to the unknown. Those of you who are wrestling with the matter of marriage—you would rather control the whole thing yourself than let God do it—because maybe God will not do it. While you are in control you can perhaps best look after your interests. What is the problem? Distrust. You talk about trusting the Lord, but you are not trusting the Lord at all; you are distrusting the Lord. You are trusting yourself and leaning on your own understanding. You believe you can do far better with yourself than ever God could. If you let yourself go fully into the hands of God He might make you a nun or a monk. On the other hand, He might bring you to the place of marriage, and for some that is worse. It is different for everybody. But while you trust yourself and remain in charge, while you have your life in your hands and you control it, you feel you are safe. At least you know yourself and you want the best for yourself. Oh, how wrong you are! Selfhood is a tyrant; there is nothing like being one's own master. And that is where you need living faith.

You cannot lose your life or fall into the ground and die of yourself. You cannot know what it is to be crucified with Christ of yourself, but at least you can come in your mind to be willing— willing to lose your life, willing to be crucified and live a crucified life, willing to take up your cross and die. But no man or woman can ever come there until they have a living, dynamic faith. You have to have that little grain of mustard-seed faith and exercise it. You do not need a lot of faith; all you need is to take that little grain of mustard seed faith, exercise it and say, "I am going to trust the Lord though He slay me. I believe God loves me. He loves me so much that He gave His Son for my life. Do I really believe that He is going to destroy me? Do I really believe that He is going to do every single thing to kill my joy, take away my peace, and make my life empty, small and little?"

This I will tell you: If you let the Lord lead you, you will know much affliction, much suffering, much brokenness, and you will go many times into death. But I will also tell you this: You will come out on the other side into *life*—which you have never known before; and *power*—which you have never known before; and an *anointing*—which you have never known before; and a *fullness*—which you have never known before. It is an infallible law with God that if you humble yourself, He will exalt you in due time. If you die with Christ you shall also live with Him. If you suffer with Him you will also be glorified with Him.

Fall Into the Ground and Die

Jesus said, *Except a grain of wheat fall into the earth and die, it abideth by itself alone; but if it die, it bringeth forth much fruit. He that loveth his life loseth it (this is in the present); and he that hateth his life in this world shall keep it unto life eternal. If any man serve me, let him follow me; and where I am there shall also my servant be* (John 12:24–26a).

"If it abideth by itself ... if it does not fall into the earth and die, it abideth by itself alone." I wonder how many people have been believers for years and are still abiding by themselves alone? As a result, there has never been a harvest. The one grain of wheat has never become two let alone ten or twenty or a hundred because it has never fallen into the earth and died.

We can pray for multiplication until our knees are sore. We can pray for men and women to be saved all around us until we are weary with prayer, but there is no substitute for falling into the earth and dying. If we are abiding by ourselves alone, it is because we have not fallen into the earth and died. What did Jesus mean? He meant this: He that saveth his life, loseth it. It is important to recognize that the Greek speaks of "soul life" or "self life". It is "psuche" from which we derive in English "psychiatry" or "psychology". When we do not lose our self life and only abide by ourself alone, we do not know the peace and the joy and the fullness and the power that the gospel proclaims. "Falleth into the ground and dies."

Wrecked Outright On Jesus' Breast

There are some people that you could place anywhere in the earth and because they know this secret it would not be long before there was a harvest. Margaret Barber once wrote a poem after there had been a shipwreck. It is a strange poem to many Christians because it seems foreign to their ears. But Margaret Barber was a servant of the Lord, who out of her own experience of falling into the ground and dying, and knowing what it was to be crucified with Christ and live with Him in newness of life, wrote this:

"Wrecked outright on Jesus' breast":
Only "wrecked" souls thus can sing;
Little boats that hug the shore,
Fearing what the storm may bring,
Never find on Jesus' breast,
All that "wrecked" souls mean by rest.

"Wrecked outright!" So we lament;
But when storms have done their worst,
Then the soul, surviving all,
In Eternal arms is nursed;
There to find that nought can move
One, embosomed in such love.

"Wrecked outright!" No more to own
E'en a craft to sail the sea;
Still a voyager, yet now
Anchored to Infinity;
Nothing left to do but fling
Care aside, and simply cling.

"Wrecked outright!" 'Twas purest gain,
Henceforth other craft can see
That the storm may be a boon,
That, however rough the sea,
God Himself doth watchful stand,
For the "wreck" is in His hand.

Now I know that this may not mean much to some, but to others it may mean a lot. There is no other way into the fullness of God than to follow the Lord Jesus, and to follow the Lord Jesus means the cross. It is the Holy Spirit by Whom we put to death the deeds of the body and Who keeps this whole matter from being turned into religion and becoming a "thing". Now if we really see what it means to be crucified with Christ then that living faith springs into action and for the first time we can reckon ourselves dead indeed unto sin but alive unto God in Christ Jesus. It is not make believe as some people try to make it, that somehow or other you can just kid yourself long enough that you are crucified and have died with Christ, and it will happen. You cannot do it. But once you see that it was in Christ that you were crucified, that it is a historical fact, and God reveals it to your heart, then for the first time you can reckon on it. You cannot let sin reign in your mortal body. May God help us in this matter.

So you want to go over into the land and possess your inheritance. You want to go over into the land and find Jerusalem. You want to go over into the land and take that Jericho that is in the way. You cannot go until first of all you know what it is to be crucified with Christ.

May God reveal this to us and lead us into a real way of life through death. The problem is not living; it is dying. People are always coming to me and saying, "Oh, I have such a problem! How can I live this Christian life?" And I always say, "That is not your problem; your problem is how to die. If you can only learn how to die, God will take care of the living. If you die, you will find that you will live. The problem is not living, it is dying."

Shall we pray:

Heavenly Father, we do pray that the Holy Spirit Himself will take over this word in its performance, preserving it from misunderstanding or misconstruction and revealing it to our hearts. There is not one of us that does not need to understand more deeply what the way of the cross really means. We pray that Thou wilt open the eyes of our hearts, and grant us that Spirit of wisdom and revelation in the knowledge of our Lord Jesus. Oh, heavenly Father, work through all our lives and in us all to bring us to the place where somehow Thou are able to do a real work in us. Oh Lord, we all want to be functioning members of the body. Show us that until the I is crucified there can be no real functioning. We want to be fruitful; show us that until we fall into the ground we abide by ourselves alone. Lord, we want to know what it is to enjoy life eternal; teach us that we cannot know life eternal in its fullness and power until we lose our lives for Thy sake and the gospel's. Open our eyes, Father, to see what Thou hast done with us in the Lord Jesus. May it come as revelation. And we ask all this in the name of our Lord Jesus. Amen.

2.
The Gateway to Life

Philippians 2:1–11

If there is therefore any exhortation in Christ, if any consolation of love, if any fellowship of the Spirit, if any tender mercies and compassions, make full my joy, that ye be of the same mind, having the same love, being of one accord, of one mind; doing nothing through faction or through vainglory, but in lowliness of mind each counting other better than himself; not looking each of you to his own things, but each of you also to the things of others. Have this mind in you, which was also in Christ Jesus: who, existing in the form of God, counted not the being on an equality with God a thing to be grasped, but emptied himself, taking the form of a servant, being made in the likeness of men; and being found in fashion as a man, he humbled himself, becoming obedient even unto death, yea, the death of the cross. Wherefore also God highly exalted him, and gave unto him the name which is above every name; that in the name of Jesus every knee should bow, of things in heaven and things on earth and things under the earth, and that every tongue should confess that Jesus Christ is Lord, to the glory of God the Father.

Romans 12:1–5

I beseech you therefore, brethren, by the mercies of God, to present your bodies a living sacrifice, holy, acceptable to God, which is your spiritual service. And be not fashioned according to this world: but be ye transformed by the renewing of your mind, that ye may prove what is the good and acceptable and perfect will of God. For I say, through the grace that was given me, to every man that is among you, not to think of himself more highly than he ought to think; but so to think as to think soberly, according as God hath dealt to each man a measure of faith. For even as we have many members in one body, and all the members have not the same office: so we, who are many, are one body in Christ, and severally members one of another.

Shall we pray:

Beloved Lord, we just want to thank You for making provision for us in every way both for the speaking and hearing of Your Word. We have already committed our time to You; and thus we want simply now to recognize that without You we can do nothing. You have provided us with that anointing grace and power, and into it we stand by faith for both the speaking of Your Word and the hearing of it. May our time together indeed be a meeting with You as You touch our hearts and challenge us, and as You encourage, correct, and fill us afresh with Your Holy Spirit. And we shall be careful to give You all the praise and glory for thus speaking to us and working amongst us. We ask all this in the name of our Lord Jesus. Amen.

I have had a certain amount of difficulty with the word for this gathering. I have no doubt about the word; just with the ability to speak it. Therefore, we are asking the Lord for it. I am sensing that the conflict over it is probably a sign of how important it is. I feel as if I have been traveling for five or six days nonstop. We were on an island in Greece and the storms came up. I was sure that there would be no boat to get us to Athens, but then it miraculously appeared in spite of the fact that we could hardly see anything due to the wind, the gale, the mist, and everything else. We made it to Jerusalem in time for the Sabbath and then found out that we had a general strike which included the airlines. They phoned us concerning our flight. I thought again that we were not going to make it after having got this far. In the meantime, I told the Lord: "You are responsible, Lord; if you want us to get to the States and if You have anything to do or to say both in myself as well as in You, You are responsible for getting us there." And then the El Al Airline phoned us and said if we could get to the airport early, they were going to bring our flight forward by so many hours which meant no sleep that night. We rushed to the airport and managed to get the flight. From then on it was a little simpler. So here we are—praise the Lord—tired and weary, but nevertheless proving the Lord's power is sufficient once again.

The Shaking Within the People of God

I wonder why it is that we have so much trouble in the fellowship of God's people. Have you ever asked yourself that? It seems incredible to me that we cannot get on together, that we are always falling out with one another, always having confrontations. It is quite extraordinary. What is the problem? It is not as if it is peculiar to you here, it seems to be peculiar to God's people everywhere. And I wonder whether, in fact, we are going to see more and more of a shaking within the people of God. It seems to me that wherever I go I hear nothing but factions, division, misrepresentation, misunderstandings and a thousand and one other things. Sometimes it is on the most ridiculous issues, so stupid that it reminds me of those problems that divided the whole Jewish community in Eastern Europe and Russia in the Middle Ages. One of those problems was focused on how many angels could stand on a pinhead. It is quite extraordinary sometimes the things that divide us. They are neither essential nor fundamental nor foundational. And one has to ask oneself: what are we going to do if Satan comes down to the earth knowing that his time is short and the atmosphere is filled with demons and evil spirits? If in a time of peace, and we could almost say tranquility, we manage to fall out with one another, what are we going to do when the real storm hits us?

Have this Mindset in You

I think the apostle Paul by the Spirit of God put his finger on it when he said: *Have this mind in you which was also in Christ*

Jesus (Philippians 2:5). You will notice that he starts by talking about being of the same mind, having the same love, being of one accord, doing nothing through faction or vainglory, but in lowliness of mind each counting the other better than himself; not looking each one to his own things but each one also to the things of others.

Then he says: Have this mind in you which was also in Christ Jesus, in the Messiah Jesus. I notice that in the New American Standard version it says: Have this "attitude" in you, or among you. I think that probably is more meaningful to the new generation, but I have to say for me it diminishes the real meaning. To have an attitude is a little different than having this mind in you which is something deeper and fuller. I almost wonder whether we could say, Have this "mindset" in you which was also in Christ Jesus. What was this mindset that was in the Messiah Jesus? He did not grasp His being on an equality with God but emptied Himself. I think that goes to the heart of the matter.

Our problem is that we are always defending our ministry, our calling, our gift, our reputation, our status. It is the most natural thing in the world in which we live, particularly in this day of human rights. Everything has to do with rights—rights of women, rights of children, rights of animals, rights of this, rights of that. Now there is nothing wrong with fighting for the rights of others, but there is something about this mentality which gets into all of us. We feel we have to be defensive or shield ourselves or we have to become a ghetto in order to protect ourselves from others.

This mindset of our Lord Jesus is altogether different. He did not grasp His being on an equality with God but emptied

Himself. One version has a footnote that says: "He laid aside all His privileges." What a blessed fellowship it would be if everyone laid aside all their privileges, and there was no fighting for status, reputation, ministry, or position, but rather that we were able to lay all these aside.

A Bondslave Without Rights

The word goes on to say: *Who, existing in the form of God, counted not the being on an equality with God a thing to be grasped, but emptied Himself, taking the form of a bondslave* (Philippians 2:6–7a)—not a household servant but a bondslave. A bondslave has no rights; he belongs to the master twenty-four hours of every day. There was nothing really, in one sense, to fight for. It is awful to think of the slavery, but it is even more remarkable to think that the Lord Jesus actually took the form of a bondslave, that is, one without any rights and without any position to have to defend, or any ministry that He felt He had to build a wall around. I find that quite amazing!

It is not as though it ends there, but it goes on to say: *Being made in the likeness of men; and being found in fashion as a man, he humbled himself, becoming obedient even unto death, yea, the death of the cross* (2:8). A person who is sentenced to death has no more rights, it is over. We have a very strange idea of carrying a cross, basically from the religious paintings that we have all grown up with according to our background. We have seen Jesus in multitudes of paintings with this huge cross over His shoulder. In Mark's gospel Jesus said: *If any man would follow me, let him give up all right to himself, deny himself, take up his cross, and follow me* (see 8:34b). The Lord Jesus was borrowing a picture here that He Himself would one day exemplify. This was a sight that was seen again and again in the crowded streets of Jerusalem in those days and, indeed, in many places throughout the Promised Land. Soldiers would go through the street shouting for people to get out of the way, and the person would follow bearing a crossbeam—not the cross but the crossbeam. The actual stake of the cross was always in position. The place of death was normally a place of public execution and the stakes were already in place. Sometimes it was an old tree trunk, and now and again it had arms; therefore there was hardly a need for the crossbeam. The person sentenced would have around his neck the sentence of death—why he had been sentenced to death. If he was wealthy he could pay a servant to carry the sentence in front of him as he went to the place of execution. When Jesus said, "If any man follow Me let him take up his cross," he meant the crossbeam. From that moment that person had within himself the sentence of death. He had no more rights, and he was on his way to the place of execution. This is an amazing picture that Jesus gave to us.

The Sentence of Death

Read it again very carefully: *If any man follows Me, let him deny himself, take up his crossbeam, and follow Me.* In other words, the actual crucifixion would take place later, but the sentence of death had been passed and that one had no further rights. That is why the Lord Jesus went on to say: *He that seeks to save his soul-life will lose it, and he that loses his soul-life for My sake and the gospel's shall save it* (see Mark 8:35). In another place it says: *"... shall find it unto life eternal"* (see John 12:25). In other words, if you are going to follow the Lord Jesus you have to take up the crossbeam; there is no such thing as discipleship without the cross.

Now we hear about the cross all the time; for we can talk endlessly about the cross, particularly in the kind of fellowships that we are in; but where is the practice? And I am not talking about laying this on someone else, thinking, "I hope so and so is listening to this." I am talking about us because we are all so deceitful. "Oh!" we say, "that is just what so and so needs, something right between the eyes. Knock them out, Lord." But we are the culprit. When we are given the opportunity to take up the crossbeam and walk to the place of execution, we fight with everything in us—for our position, for our character, for our reputation, our ministry, or whatever else. *This* is the problem.

You may ask this question: "Who is going to do the crucifying?" There is certainly no problem there! Your dearest and nearest will willingly do it. The executioners are manifold—your husband, wife, children, parents, colleagues at work, and failing all else, the church itself. There is no paucity of executioners; it is the sentence of death. Jesus did not say, "If any man wants to be greatly used let him deny himself, take up his cross and follow me." Nor did He say, "If any man wants to be something in the kingdom let him deny himself, take up his cross and follow me." Of course, this is true, but He never said it. He said, "If any man follows Me." Now that means if you and I are not giving up all rights to ourselves and taking up the crossbeam, we are not following Jesus. We may be following some doctrine—not that I despise good and sound doctrine—but we may be following a concept or a kind of idea of Christianity or some idea of being spiritual, but it is not the following of the Lord Jesus. Nobody can follow the Lord Jesus and escape the cross. It stands in the way. It is one of the great ironies of faith. We are saved by the work of the Lord Jesus on the cross, but once we are saved we can only know the fullness of our salvation and the realistic practical outworking of our salvation by denying self and taking up the crossbeam.

The Agents of Our Crucifixion

Now this is our problem because if it were only angels who did the crucifying we would have a good time. We would feel somehow or other that this would be a wonderful thing. These angels would sort of gently put our hands on the crossbeam and tie them to the stake. Then they would spiritually anesthetize us as they drove the nails through our hands. But it is not angels who do it. It is the world, it is your nearest and dearest, and it is the church. And that is our problem because we are scandalized by the thought that people in the church could be our executioners! It is unbelievable for you to think of your husband, your wife, your parents, or your children as the executioners. These very people that we think should be sweet and loving are the ones who are the agents of our being crucified. Our fellowship, our family life, our home life, our business life would be transformed if we gave up all right to ourselves and took up the crossbeam.

Sometimes people ask the Lord if they might live a crucified life, but they are not very happy when they discover that it is their brothers and sisters who crucify them. Is this not a strange anomaly? You may think it is ridiculous to consider anything like this; but what do you think crucifixion is? Do you think it is a sweet ecstasy? Do you think it is something beautiful? It is something bloody and unrelenting. I think for all of us the biggest shock is the people that God uses to bring us to the place of death.

The apostle says in his second letter to the Corinthians: *We have the sentence of death within ourselves, that we should not trust in ourselves, but in God who raises the dead* (see II Corinthians 1:9). In other words, you can crucify me but my faith is in God that He will raise me up in newness of life. In the end we will become thankful for the very people who are the agents of our crucifixion. Now this kind of word may not be quite so comforting to us, but there is no other way to walk in newness of life, to know resurrection life, or to know church life than this way.

Have this mindset in you (amongst yourselves) *which was also in the Messiah Jesus: who, being in the form of God, did not count being on an equality with God a thing to be grasped* (see Philippians 2:6). That mean little thing—our reputation or that stupid position we are fighting for pales into insignificance beside what the Lord Jesus could have fought for: "being in the form of God, counted not being on an equality with God a thing to be grasped." If the Lord Jesus did not grasp such a divine position, such a totally right position, where does that leave you and me? What is wrong with us? What are we fighting for? When we fight for our rights, we not only destroy ourselves, we destroy others.

The Perfect Church?

When we are young in the Lord, many of us think of the church as the most wonderful community of saints. I remember when

I was first saved I thought that it was the most wonderful thing I had ever been in—all those dear people with their shining faces. Within a few years I discovered the ugliness in them all, and the bottom fell out of my Christian life as a result. I remember the pastor was so horrified when I went off to stay with an uncle and aunt in Paris. He got them to pray for me because he thought it would be the end of my going on with the Lord. I was only sixteen at the time; therefore, he felt that going to Paris which he considered such an evil place—a cesspool of wickedness and iniquity—would finish me. And I wrote a letter, not to the pastor but to the deaconess who was a very dear lady and loved the Lord. However, she was very irritated by my letter which was full of complaints about the whole assembly from the pastor down. "The deacons," I said, "never come to the prayer meeting, they are all too busy." And then I had complaints about this and that and the other and the fact that the young people's class was not young people. We had a young women's Bible class. Most of them were 75 or older. They had grown up with it but were then left on the shelf! She was so mortified by my letter that she took it to the pastor and he gave it to the deacons. I was only letting off steam and I thought that maybe this would force her to her knees to pray. The fact is that the bottom had fallen out of my life with regard to believers being the most wonderful people. We had two pastors and it was like two great factions in the church because they fought each other the whole time. Of course they all sang wonderful hymns such as: "My chains fell off" and others like it, but it was pretty clear to me that the chains were very much there.

Then I got a letter back from this dear sister to say what she had done—and it was a very cold letter—I really felt the end had come. And I said out loud: "Lord, I could not care less about your people, I am finished with them. They are such a rag-tag bag of non-descripts." And I remember clearly a voice behind me saying, "You can give them up, but can you give Me up?" It was so real that I swung round as if there was someone there, and then I realized it was the Lord. I said: "I cannot give you up!" It was like Christian in *Pilgrim's Progress* when he was crossing the last river and he sank, crying out: "Help me, save me!" Then, suddenly, his feet touched the bottom and he said, "It is all right; I have touched the bottom." That was the moment when I turned the corner and from then on it did not matter if every one of God's people was a liar or unrealistic, or unreal or anything else, my life was built on the Lord Jesus Himself. I could not give Him up.

If you expect a lot from God's people, I wonder if you have ever thought about yourself. Let me put it another way: How did the Lord receive you? Was it as a fully-fledged holy saint? No, it was not. Did He receive you as a person full of determination to go to the very end? No, I do not think He did. Did He receive you as someone who was prepared to lay down one's life for Him? No, He did not. How did He receive you? It was as a worthless, ugly, sinner. If anyone thinks that the Lord saved you because you were so sweet, then that is what the church is for—to tear away that façade. Everybody is looking for the perfect church; but where is the perfect church? I was saved when I was thirteen years of age and I am now quite old, but I have never found the perfect church. I have only found elitist groups all huddled on some particular doctrinal truth. There is no such thing as a perfect church! The church, to be the church, has to be imperfect here on earth, and the Lord uses it to bring us face to face with reality. How did the Lord receive us as sinners? We had absolutely no claim on Him. We were sinners bound for hell and a lost eternity, and He saved us through His unlimited grace. We did not deserve anything. If we think we did, the Lord has to do a bit more work in us.

When the apostle Paul wrote his first letter, he said he was the "least of all saints" (see Ephesians 3:8). But when he wrote his last letter, he called himself the "chief of all sinners" (see 1 Timothy 1:16). The more he went on with the Lord, the more he realized that he was only saved by the grace of God which he did not deserve.

God has so designed the church that every façade you have will be destroyed by your brothers and sisters. Why fight? It is the very design of the house of God. Of course, there is something wonderful happening. Gold, silver, and precious stones are being produced; but the Lord uses the members of the body of Christ to destroy all our fantasies and to bring us face to face with reality.

Wash One Another's Feet

Have this mindset in you, which was also in the Messiah Jesus: who being in the form of God, did not think that equality with God was a thing to be grasped, fought over, but emptied Himself and became a bondslave. "Oh," someone says, "surely there should be holiness in the church." You are dead right, there should be holiness in the church but, unfortunately, most of us by nature are extremely unholy. "Oh," you say, "we cannot have anything to do with unholiness!" Of course not, but may I remind you that our Lord Jesus, on the night in which He was betrayed, actually took a towel and a basin of water and washed the disciples' feet (see John 13:4–5). "Well," you say, "that is wonderful; it is a beautiful picture." Every one of those disciples, whose feet He washed, were going to deny Him. Would we have done that? No, we would not have done that. We would have said: "I am not washing so-and-so's feet, that person is going to deny me with oaths three times! Out!" But you say, "We have to be gracious." Yes, that is true, but then what about Judas? He washed the feet of Judas, who was a thief as well as a betrayer. And then Jesus said: "I have left you an example."

What is the problem about washing one another's feet? Feet are not only the smelliest part of us, generally speaking, they are not the most beautiful part. Why did the Lord leave such an example to us? You might say: "He should have shown more discernment. I am only having fellowship with people who do not have smelly feet."

We all have our feet on this earth, and our Lord Jesus said: "The proof of your discipleship is whether or not you can wash one another's feet." Have this mindset in you which was also in the Messiah Jesus, Who being in the form of God did not think equality with God a thing to be grasped but humbled Himself. Here is God the Son, through whom all things were created, and for whom all things were created, and in whom all things hold together, washing the feet of a lot of disciples who were going to fail Him without exception. Does that not cut across all our arguments of not having anything to do with ones who have smelly feet?

An Advanced Working Party

Let me put it another way. There is an idea that the church is exclusive. Of course there is a right sense in which the church is exclusive. Everyone who is not born again is outside of it. Nevertheless, the church, by its very nature, is inclusive. Everyone who is born of God, no matter what name they go by, if they are born of God, they are in Christ. And if they are in Christ, they are in the church—whether Catholic, Orthodox, Southern Baptist, Presbyterian, Brethren, and even exclusives. If they are born of God they are in Christ. And if they are not born of God they are excluded—not from the grace of God, not from the mercy of God, not from the love of God—from the church.

This wonderful truth is something incredible. I often use the illustration of the exiles in trying to explain it. Those who went back to Jerusalem were such a tiny minority. They went back to the land in three waves and rebuilt the house of God and the walls of Jerusalem. They rebuilt all the cities. In fact, the very prophecies of Isaiah, of Micah, and of others could not have been fulfilled but for this tiny minority within the whole community of God's people. If they had not gone back the very prophetic Scriptures would not have been fulfilled nor would the Messiah have been born in Bethlehem. There was no Bethlehem, no Nazareth, no Capernaum; they had been destroyed. There was no temple in which the Lord could suddenly appear according to Malachi (3:1). The Lord used that small group, but never at any point did those who went back divide themselves from those who remained in the Diaspora! They would not touch the fact that they remained in the Diaspora, which was wrong, but as Brother Sparks used to say, "They were an advanced working party." They went back so that the rest could come into the salvation of God. And in the end, three times a year, all the people from the Diaspora would go up to Jerusalem.

What I am trying to say very simply is this: When we see what the church is and we stand in Christ, we will receive every born-again believer. They are part of us and we are part of them. We are not going to touch what is wrong, but we will never divide ourselves from the people of God who are in denominations and all the other institutional things. They are still ours and we belong to them. Otherwise, we become exclusive and a divider of the body of our Lord Jesus.

If a Cardinal comes to me in the Catholic Church and he is born of God, I have to receive him. I very well remember being asked to go to Lambeth Palace in London, the residence of the Archbishop of Canterbury, to a gathering of Christian leaders of all kinds to talk about the spiritual condition of the country. And I remember that the Archbishop, who was an evangelical and really preached the gospel, gave an address and it was as dead as a door nail—absolutely lifeless. When he finished he said, "I would like to call on Cardinal Hume to come forward and pray for us." And Basil Hume got up and walked forward and fell on his knees, lifted up his hands, and heaven opened. This was the man who led Malcolm Muggeridge, the greatest atheist of the twentieth century in Britain, to the Lord. Now what do you do? He was not only a Catholic but a Cardinal. What more can you ask? We cannot touch the thing, but that man is a brother. He has been received by Christ; can I reject him?

It is one of the hardest things in the world to not touch what is wrong but to receive a brother and a sister as those received by the Lord. Then what are we doing together? Why do we not all go back into whatever we came out of? It is because we believe that the house of God has to be built and there is a remnant of those who, like the ones who went back to Jerusalem, have to go back by the grace of God and power of the Holy Spirit to rebuild the temple and walls of Jerusalem so that the purpose of God and the Word of God might be fulfilled. We are an advanced working party for the rest. We shall find them all in the end, but it was those who went back who were directly involved in the coming of the Messiah, not those who remained in the dispersion or the exile. They had comfortable homes and comfortable lives; they had synagogues, places of worship, places of Bible study and much else, but the purpose of God and the Word of God could not be fulfilled in the exile.

Now the problem is that all those who go back are not so sweet and pure. We have as many executioners among the remnant who go back as there are in the exile, ready to nail us to the cross. So why do we fight this?

Humility and Brokenness

It says, *Wherefore also God hath highly exalted Him* (Philippians 2:9a). It is a principle with God; we go down into death, God will take care of the resurrection. The deeper we go down, the higher we will reach. The way to greatness is through humility and the way to being filled with the power and glory of God is brokenness; it is so simple. We all know it, but it is the process that we do not like. If only it was ugly, wicked sinners who were martyring us, but it is the Lord's people. We can even accept unsaved people being part of the execution, but when it is the Lord's people, we find it so hard. Then everything within us rises up to defend ourselves, our ministry, our status, our character, everything. But there are no rights in death, that is the gateway to life.

The Renewing of the Mind

The apostle says again in Romans: *I beseech you therefore, brethren, by the mercies of God, to present your bodies a living sacrifice, holy, acceptable to God which is your spiritually intelligent worship* (12:1). Spiritually intelligent worship is to be a living sacrifice. And what did they do with these sacrifices? They were placed on the altar and slain, and they went up in smoke. That is not quite what we were expecting or what we want. But the Word goes on to say, *And do not be fashioned according to this world: but be ye transformed by the renewing of your mind* (12:2a). "Be transformed by the renewing of your mind." If you have an old mind you will be fashioned according to this world. It is only by being transformed through the renewing of your mind that you can prove what is the good and perfect and acceptable will of God. We cannot find the will of God acceptable apart from being transformed by the renewing of our mind. But when that happens through being a living sacrifice, then everything else follows. We suddenly discover the body, and that we are members one of another. We are members first and foremost in the Lord Jesus, the Messiah Himself. Then we discover that we are members one of another. Just as it says in Romans, *Receive ye one another, even as Christ also received you, to the glory of God* (15:7), you and I begin to receive one another on the minimal basis of being a sinner saved by grace. Then we are no longer shocked, "Oh! Did you hear about so and so? I never thought they were capable of such a thing!" I have come to realize that the children of God are capable of anything. I have none of these big ideas that they are not capable, they are capable of anything. But God in His grace has saved us and whilst we do not become partakers of one another's sins, nevertheless we receive one another as Christ also received me and you.

May the Lord help us. We are now moving into days when we are going to see more and more demonic activity. I believe that the United States is the last bulwark against the coming of the Antichrist. It would not surprise me if in the next few years you see a flood of evil submerge the country and then the last great bulwark against the coming of the Antichrist will have been swept away. Whatever you may feel about your President [George W. Bush], he seems to me to be a child of God. He prays more than some Christians I know, and I heard a story the other day of someone who came into the Oval Office and found him on his face before God. Whether he understands some of the things from the Word of God that he ought to understand I do not know. But once he goes and America loses her superpower status, we will see evil in a way that we have never seen it before.

The Top Stone Will Be Put in Place

How are we going to go on? How are we going to remain together? How are we going to see the house of God completed? It is true that according to Zechariah, when the top stone comes forth, they will only be able to shout—but they will shout: "Grace, grace unto it" (see Zechariah 4:7). It was the grace of God that began this work, the grace of God that developed it and preserved it, and the grace of God that will complete it. So in the midst of breakdown, evil, darkness and the coming of the Antichrist, the top stone will come into its place. The top stone, of course, is the Lord Jesus, just as He is the foundation, the chief corner stone, and the head of the corner. He is everything.

How are we going to stay together? How are we going to go through together? Shall we hive off into elite little groups? I must tell you that these little elite groups—and I have seen so many of them through my life—never last. They are so elite that they always find some who are not so elite and out they go and then a few more, and out they go another way. We need to be of the same mind and the same love, doing nothing through vainglory. We need to have this mind in us which was also in the Messiah Jesus. May the Lord challenge us.

And you do not need to go to somebody that you have had a problem with and say to them, "I have had a dreadful problem with you. You have no idea what you have done to me over these years." I have seen this many, many times. We say, "Please forgive me, I have such problem with you because I think you are so ugly and so dark and so arrogant and proud, but the Lord has given me repentance." Do not do that, it is a back-hander. We need to humble ourselves before the Lord.

The Word of God tells us to humble ourselves. Do not wait to be humbled. That is terrible; it is like a great stone that falls upon you and grinds you to dust. It is better to get on your knees and say, "Lord, forgive me, I have been expecting *too* much, criticizing, murmuring, and all the rest of it. Forgive me. Help me to get clear, help me to be part of the building, help me to be part of that remnant that will go right through to glory." Could there be anything more wonderful than in the end to hear the Lord say: "Well done, good and faithful servant"? May the Lord help us and give us this mindset that was in the Messiah Jesus.

Shall we pray:

Lord, we are pretty poor material when it comes to it—all of us. But in Your mercy You have saved us. And sometimes, Lord, we have problems with one another's poverty of character or of holiness or whatever. Would You challenge us not to think of others but to think of ourselves? Help us, Lord, to humble ourselves before Your mighty hand, that You may exalt us in due season. Lord, hear us. May this word be saved and preserved from any misunderstanding of any kind. Bring it home to us with all the power of Your anointing so that we cannot escape it. We want to follow You. We want to go the whole way, Lord. Will You do something in our lives that delivers us from all this criticism and judgment of one another in a wrong way? Deliver us, oh Lord, from this spirit of the world and this spirit from hell, and renew us in such a way by becoming living sacrifices. Renew us and transform us by the renewing of our mind that we may be able to prove what is that good and perfect and acceptable will of Yours. Hear us, Lord, we pray, for we ask this in the name of our Lord Jesus. Amen.

3.
They Loved Not Their Life Even Unto Death

Revelation 12:7–11

And there was war in heaven: Michael and his angels going forth to war with the dragon; and the dragon warred and his angels; and they prevailed not, neither was their place found any more in heaven. And the great dragon was cast down, the old serpent, he that is called the Devil and Satan, the deceiver of the whole world; he was cast down to the earth, and his angels were cast down with him. And I heard a great voice in heaven, saying, Now is come the salvation, and the power, and the kingdom of our God, and the authority of his Messiah: for the accuser of our brethren is cast down, who accuseth them before our God day and night. And they overcame him because of the blood of the Lamb, and because of the word of their testimony; and they loved not their life even unto death.

II Corinthians 5:14–15

For the love of Christ constraineth us; because we thus judge, that one died for all, therefore all died; and he died for all, that they that live should no longer live unto themselves, but unto him who for their sakes died and rose again.

Ephesians 3:9
And to make all men see what is the dispensation of the mystery which for ages hath been hid in God who created all things.
(... the stewardship or dispensation of the mystery)

Colossians 1:26–27
Even the mystery which hath been hid for ages and generations; but now hath it been manifested to his saints, to whom God was pleased to make known what is the riches of the glory of this mystery among the Gentiles, which is Christ in you, the hope of glory.

Colossians 2:2–3
That their hearts may be comforted, they being knit together in love, and unto all riches of the full assurance of understanding, that they may know the mystery of God, even Christ, in whom are all the treasures of wisdom and knowledge hidden.

A word of prayer:

Beloved Lord, we are so thankful that we are found here in Your presence, and we are thankful that You are actually more interested in our gathering together than we are sometimes to gather together. Nevertheless, by Your Holy Spirit You can somehow work in our hearts through this word. We all know much of the truth; it is in our hearts and minds but, Lord, the reality is not there very often.

Only the Holy Spirit can illumine our hearts and our spirits and cause us to understand through revelation what it all is about. Hear us, Lord. We thank You for the anointing which You have so dearly won for us at Calvary. Into that anointing power and grace we stand by faith both for the speaker, for the translator and for the hearer. Lord, let this be an anointed time when we really meet with You; and we ask it in the name of our Lord Jesus. Amen.

We are considering this matter, "they overcame"—they overcame Satan. And notice that we have three constituents in overcoming. *They overcame Satan because of* (or very simply in the Greek, *through*) *the blood of the Lamb; and because of* (or *by reason of,* or *through*) *the word of their testimony, and they loved not their lives even unto death.* Some versions actually put a definite article before death: *And they loved not their lives even unto the death.*

The Truth of Doctrine Made Real in Jesus

It is interesting that the first two constituents of overcoming are set in a certain way, but the last is quite different. It is almost as if the Holy Spirit is saying: "This last constituent has to underlie the other two or there will be no reality. It will be sham. There will be profession, there will be religion, there will be words, there will be doctrine, there will be knowledge, but there will be no reality." Now it is very interesting that this word *truth* in the Word of God, which immediately brings to most of us thoughts of doctrine, of words, of teaching in the Holy Scriptures—and it does cover these things— this word in Greek means "reality." It is not just the truth of doctrine as it is in Jesus, as good and sound as it is which is important, but it is the reality as it is in Jesus. When the Lord Jesus said: *I am the way, the truth and the life,* He was saying: *I am the way, the "reality" and the life* (see John 14:6a). Now if we do not have that reality, where are we? It is simply religion or profession without the experience which is so vital. Only the Holy Spirit can take the doctrine and the teaching and pierce our hearts.

Those of you who have been brought up in deeply religious Christian homes must have experienced knowing *about* the Lord. But surely there came a day when what you knew from babyhood suddenly dawned on you, and in that moment you were saved and born of the Spirit. You had heard it all, it was all "old hat," and you could almost preach it yourself as a child or as an adolescent, but the fact is that when that truth became reality, from that moment you were born of God. It was different, and you entered a new dimension, a new world; it was a new creation. The other was something outside, but when the Holy Spirit, by the grace of God, touched your heart you were saved. There are no second-generation Christians. There are no grandchildren with God, He has only children. There is something absolutely direct and absolutely original about the Lord.

The Blood of the Martyrs Has Been the Seed of the Church

Let us look a little more closely at this extraordinary word: *And they overcame Satan through the blood of the Lamb and through the word of their testimony, and they loved not their lives even unto death.* Is it martyrdom that is in view here? There is absolutely no doubt whatsoever that the old saying from the church fathers is true: "The blood of the martyrs is the seed of the church." Wherever believers have died in their faith or have been martyred for their testimony, before long something has happened. Think of the Anabaptists who were drowned by their thousands. There is not a single fountain or pool in the city of Salzburg, Austria that did not see men, women, and children tied up in sacks, weighed down with rocks, and flung into those fountains and pools and drowned. But an amazing thing happened. The Baptists have gone everywhere and it has become one of the biggest denominations in Christianity. It may be pretty unrealistic at times, but the fact of the matter is that it is everywhere. The blood of the martyrs has been the seed of the church.

We think of the followers of Jan Huss, the Czech reformer, who was tricked by the Catholics in going to Constance for a dialogue with the Catholic leaders, and was instead burned there at the stake. His followers throughout Bohemia and Moravia, throughout what we now call the Czech Republic, throughout the southern parts of Germany and all of Austria, died in their thousands. However, out of the blood of the martyrs came the Moravian church which was one of the most extraordinary eras in the history of the true church. Those people went everywhere with the gospel. They actually sold themselves as slaves in order to be with the slaves and win them to the Lord Jesus. They contracted leprosy whilst looking after lepers and then became missionaries to the lepers. They went to the Eskimos in the arctic, they even went into Tibet, the high roof of the world. The story of the Moravians is incredible and deeply moving!

One could go on and on with this matter of martyrdom, for wherever you look, wherever believers have died and been murdered for their faith for holding the testimony of Jesus, there have, in the end, been results. Today, we see it in mainland China, in perhaps the greatest ethnic group of believers in the world. The martyrs' blood has become the seed of the church.

I remember years ago, when I was in Egypt staying with two old missionaries who had such an influence on my life. I had never seen such a prayer ministry. Although I had been in wonderful prayer meetings and had seen wonderful answers to prayer, I had never seen anything like Alexandra Liblik and Kathleen Smythe. I only got to be with them because I was very ill. For a month or two I had been in the hospital on my back, not even allowed to put a foot down on the ground. When I was finally released from the Royal Air Force Hospital, the medics said, "You have to go on convalescence for at least three weeks' rest, and we will pay for it." And I said to Susan Hamill, the wife of the Superintendent of the Egypt General Mission's Ismailiya station: "I do not know where I can go for three weeks." She replied: "Leave it to me. There are two old godly missionaries that are retired in Port Said. I will phone them." After phoning them she came back to me and said: "I have arranged it. They are expecting you at any time, so just go." But then she said to me: "Just remember, you are a very young man of eighteen, very arrogant and straight in what you say. These are very godly and pious missionaries, so be very careful."

I found out that these very godly and pious missionaries had had exactly the same experience as myself, and we became the greatest of friends. Then one day I said to Alexandra Liblik, "You have been in Egypt for fifty years and have hardly left this country except for a month's holiday in the mountains. How many converts have you had?" She lifted up her hand and said, "Five." And I said, "Is it worth it?" She replied: "One day there will be an enormous harvest from Islam." That harvest has come. My friends in Athens cannot keep abreast of the number of Muslims that are turning to the Lord from Indonesia, Pakistan, Afghanistan, and Kurdistan. In these Islamic areas, for the first time since the seventh century, Muslims are turning to the Lord Jesus. They are having extraordinary visions and dreams, sometimes even visions in the daytime, and they hear voices that speak to them out of the heavens. Whole families are turning to the Lord. I have never seen anything like it. And it is all the result of Muslim savagery to Muslims and the murder of Muslims who have become Christians. We hear it again and again when we ask: "What started you on this journey to the Lord?" They reply: "I saw brother so and so; they chopped off one arm and told him to say the Koranic Creed and he would not; then they chopped off his other arm and decapitated him." The blood of the martyrs is the seed of the church, but is that really what this verse says?

Laying Down Our Self-Life

And they loved not their life even unto death. Do you know anyone who has given his or her life for the sake of the Lord and the gospel who has not first laid down their self-life? It would be quite extraordinary to be prepared to die physically for the Lord if you had never first laid down your self-life, because the deepest instinct in the human being is self-preservation. God knew what He was doing when He said: "Thou shalt love thy neighbor as thyself." We all love ourselves—we try to protect ourselves, we want to expand ourselves, we strive to advance ourselves, and we seek self-glory. We seek status for ourselves and titles before our name, degrees after our name, anything that gives us the feeling that we are successful in ourselves. If you should come to the point where you are challenged with either death or the denial of the Lord Jesus, most of us would deny the Lord Jesus—unless we had not first laid down our self-life. Hence that extraordinary passage in II Corinthians 5:14–15: *For the love of Christ constraineth us; because we thus judge, that one died for all, therefore all died; and he died for all, that they that live should no longer live unto themselves, but unto him who for their sakes died and rose again.*

Jesus Died For Us

Four or five days ago I woke up in the middle of the night with this verse running through my head. What an incredible word this is: *He (that is, Jesus) died for all, therefore, all have died. And He died for all, that they that live should not live unto themselves but for Him who for their sakes died and rose again.* This is the other side of the gospel. Jesus died for us; He died in our place; He bore the punishment of our sin in His body on the tree. He never flinched but went forward and endured it all for us.

Jesus Died As You

However, there is another side. He not only died for you, He died *as you. He died for all, therefore, all have died.* Dr. Martin Lloyd

Jones used to say: "Take great note of the small prepositions—*"but,"* *"to," "for," "wherefore," "therefore;"* these kinds of words." Again, *He died for all, therefore all have died.* As far as God is concerned, if you are a child of God, Jesus died for you and you died with Him. Therefore, those of us who are alive on this earth should live unto Him.

They Loved Not Their Self-Life

In the passage that we are considering in Revelation 12 it says, "… and they loved not their life even unto death." Now the word there for life is *psuche* from which we get psychiatry and psychology. It is the soul. Therefore we can read this verse like this: "And they loved not their soul-life even unto death." Or "They loved not their self-life even unto the death." Who does not love their self-life? Even those of us who spend our whole time saying how poor we are, how hopeless we are, how ugly we are, and how impossible it is for anything to happen with us—it is only an inverted way of pumping ourselves up. "Poor me, I have inherited so much from my parents, grandparents and my great grandparents. Have mercy on me—my poor little self." No, we do not have a little self at all, we have a *big* self. It wants to get out into the open, to advance, to expand, to get status, and be thought of highly. This is our self-life, is it not?

Do not all the problems in the believer's life come from this self-life? We know what to do with sins, we know that Jesus died for our sins. We know that the blood of the Lord Jesus washes us clean. We know that if we confess our sin He is faithful and just to forgive us our sin and to cleanse us from all unrighteousness (see I John 1:9). There is no problem with sin; the sin and the sinning problem have been dealt with. The problem is with the self-life. We can be forgiven and our sins canceled out, but our self-life can be vibrant, energetic, in full force and power. This is the problem in the believer's life. It says, *They overcame Satan by the blood of the Lamb—by the finished work of the Lord Jesus.* This full salvation through the finished and completed work of the Lord Jesus has been given to us by God. We do not have to pay for it, we do not have to do good works for it; it is given to us by the grace of God, "For by grace have ye been saved through faith; and that not of yourselves, it is the gift of God" (Ephesians 2:8).

But what do we do about our self-life? That is the thing that stops us from experiencing the fullness of His salvation. That is the condition that completely destroys any growth in the Lord. It paralyzes us. It stops us from moving forward and advancing in the Lord. It is exactly the same with the church. We get a whole collection of "I's" together and we have problems: "I think, I feel, I know, I want, I will." What a problem we have!

What about the work of the Lord? When there are a few brothers and sisters together who are gifted, before long there are rivalries and jealousies. They are too spiritual to talk about it, but the jealousies are deep down within and eventually they will be manifested: "So and so seems to be getting further on than me, he seems to be more successful than me, she seems to make more impact than me."

The Success Syndrome

The American scene is amazing for us in the Old World because it is built on the success principle. Anyone who has ability can be a success, which is simply amazing for us in the Old World where so much depends upon the old-school tie, the blood-line, background, pedigree, and where and how you were educated. It is better now but in the old days a person could not get very far regardless of how successful or able a person was because of this bondage to class. The problem however with the success syndrome is that when you begin to gather together a few believers, before long attitudes surface such as: "I want to minister, I want to lead, I want this." It is the self-life.

And they loved not their life even unto death. Living for self or living for Christ—it is so simple. *He died for all, therefore all died; and He died for all, that they who live should not live unto themselves*—for the advancement of their self-lives—*but should live for Him who for their sakes died and rose again.*

Many Converts—Few Disciples

Let us be honest. This question of reality is our biggest problem. I am glad it has come up because we are very near to the coming of the Lord. If you and I are not prepared for the Lord to deal with our self-life we will discover that there is no reward and no "well done" from the Lord. Our problem in Christian circles is very simple. We have made thousands of converts and very few disciples. Jesus never said, *Go ye therefore into the world and make converts of all nations.* He said, *Go ye into all the world and make disciples of all the nations.* No one can be a disciple who has not laid down their self-life. If my self-life is intact—Christianized, singing hymns, saying prayers, reading the Bible, all outward—it is a great sham and the reality is not there. The reality is only when I surrender my will to the Lord Jesus.

Knowing Him

This matter of the will is the biggest single issue in any child of God. Our will, our reasoning powers, and emotions are all centered in our soul—our psuche, our self-life—so it is only natural for us to somehow or other try to look as if we are moving on with the Lord when the truth is quite different. We are advancing in knowledge and not in experience. Reality is when you grow in grace and in the knowledge of the Lord Jesus Christ as the apostle Peter said (see II Peter 3:18). That knowledge is not just knowing things, truths, and doctrines but it is knowing Him. When you get to know Him, the doctrine is right as well. The Lord Jesus will see to that and so will the Holy Spirit.

The Obstacle to Reality

The great obstacle to reality is an unbroken, uncrucified self-life. It destroys all progress, all growth, all transformation into the likeness of the Lord Jesus, and all fruitfulness. It means there is no power; therefore, we have to make up for it with noise. The real power is not there. It is an obstacle to experiencing everything that Jesus has won for you.

When I used to travel all over the world, the most common question I was asked by young people was: "How can I live the Christian life?" And I always answered them in the same way: "That is not the question you should ask. The question is not how to live the Christian life but how to die. If you learn to die with Christ, the Christian life will take care of itself. It will blossom and grow and bear fruit. Everything that you need in gifting will come to the surface once you are prepared to die with Christ." Then the question is asked: "How do you die with Christ?" Now you do not have to worry your head about that because your dear ones will do it for you. If you have a wife, a husband, children, parents, business colleagues, they will do it for you. And if you are in the church, they will certainly do it for you. Let me tell you, you do not have to worry your head about dying. The experience of being crucified with Christ is all there, and it is in the hands of the Lord.

People seem to have an idea that they are going to have some wonderful, ecstatic, spiritual experience when an angel visits them, takes their hand, kisses it, and nails it to the cross. He then takes a silver nail and with a golden hammer taps it in. He kisses the other hand and nails it to the cross, and you will then be filled with euphoria and a wonderful ecstatic feeling of paradise! There is no such experience! Once you are prepared to die with Christ, the Holy Spirit will take care of your crucifixion within hours. You will discover that you have a situation where you either defend yourself or you die. The Lord is in this business. You cannot set up a school for this or give three steps or a methodology; it is the Holy Spirit's work. That is why this whole matter of reality is tied intimately with the person of the Holy Spirit. He leads you into all truth. He takes of the things of the Lord Jesus and makes them real to you. It is the work of the Holy Spirit. When we quench the Holy Spirit or grieve Him, we have done something terribly damaging to ourselves.

I am sorry that this sounds so heavy, but what else can I do? The verse does not say, "And there is abundant blessing." It says, "And you have to die." Of course, someone always says, "But is this not all to do with martyrdom?" That person is trying to get out of it by thinking: "I think this is all to do with being a martyr, and I will never be a martyr." However, we will never be a martyr unless first we lay down our self-life. That is the way.

Holding the Testimony of Jesus

This obstacle of one's self-life will always keep us from the reality of holding the testimony of Jesus, thus we shall never know real church life, or what it is to be built together, or what it is to see men and women coming into our midst and touching the presence of God and being saved. We shall never know what it is to be the home of God on this earth. Every human being is looking for home; it is within us. It is a homing instinct which was planted within us at the very beginning of time and the church is to be that home. We are homeless without God. He alone is our home and when God can build the house of the Lord, that becomes His home. Immediately, the world touches something it has not touched before—something of love, grace, self-sacrifice. This could change the whole world if only it was experienced in reality!

The obstacle to holding the testimony of Jesus is my self-life and your self-life. There is no reality when our self-life is unbroken and uncrucified; there is only a façade, only words, only profession, only religion. The gateway to reality is therefore utter simplicity; it is to die. If you are prepared to die with Christ, the Holy Spirit will take care of the resurrection.

"Oh," you say, "take away my self-life—the music, the artistry, the creativity, the genius in my soul? Crucify it? Lose it? Is this the gospel?" But you lose it to receive it back under new management. You may not get back everything but you may get back much. I am sure you probably know this. One person plays the piano and you think: "Isn't that person clever." Another person plays the piano and you are in the presence of the Lord. One person sings a hymn and you think: "Nice, voice; clever." Another person sings and you are in the presence of the Lord, face to face with Him. One person preaches and you think: "Wow! He has got great knowledge, that was so good. That was like an encyclopedic message on theology." But another person preaches and you are face to face with the Lord. Reality is only when God gets what He wants in you. But there is a problem.

Handing Jesus the Keys of Our Self-Life

Mr. Sparks used to say: "The Holy Spirit is a perfect Gentleman. He never barges in or blasts you. He waits for you to hand Him the keys of your self-life." Strangely, that is the thing that most of us find so difficult to do. We will do anything else—run a marathon for the Lord, walk a thousand miles, preach until we are blue in the face, do a thousand things for the Lord, but to give Him the keys of our self-life—never!

The Lordship of Jesus

It is the will that is the problem. I will put it another way that you may be able to understand better; it is the Lordship of Jesus. We can all say, "You are Lord." Is He? Could He really speak to you and tell you to go somewhere or to do this or that or give up this? Is He Lord? Or is He Lord in name only?

When I had to speak a few years ago in Britain, in Leicester (which is now largely a Muslim city with the prayer call echoing over the whole city), I preached in Melbourne Hall which was founded by Dr. F. B. Meyer. The pastor said to me at the end of it: "You have been standing in the pulpit where C. T. Studd stood on the day he left for China. He was a young man, a graduate of Cambridge University, and he was going out with six others to China. Afterwards, Dr. F. B. Meyer said to him in the vestry: 'What is the secret of your ministry and of your life?'" And C. T. Studd thought for a moment and then said: "My secret is that I have surrendered my will to the Lord." C. T. fell into the ground and died. He went out to China, from there he went to India, and from India he went to the Congo where he died. He never returned to Britain. He said: "Missionaries do not go on furlough." Out of that came a tremendous fellowship of missionaries. Such is what can happen with a human being's life when they surrender their will. Would you believe that such a small thing, or something that may seem so small to you, could lead to a whole universe of experience and understanding and wisdom? But so it is with the Lord. He asks you: "Am I really Lord of your life? You call me Lord, but am I Lord? Am I really responsible for you and your life? Are you ready to obey Me in whatever I might say?" Only the Lord can help you.

Shall we pray:

Beloved Lord, we very simply commit ourselves to You. This self-life of ours is a problem. It is something like an octopus with so many tentacles. We cut off one and then discover we have got seven others. And Lord, we hardly know what to do other than this: "You died for all, therefore, all died that those who live might not live unto themselves, but unto You who for our sake died and rose again." Lord, have dealings with us. Do not let us go on in this way. If we refuse to give You our will, it means that we are relegated to a life of sham, of unreality, of simply religious observance without the real experience of Yourself. Deal with us, Lord, by Your Holy Spirit. We ask it in the name of Jesus. Amen.

4.
If Any Man Follow Me

Revelation 12:10–11

And I heard a great voice in heaven, saying, Now is come the salvation, and the power, and the kingdom of our God, and the authority of his Messiah: for the accuser of our brethren is cast down, who accuseth them before our God day and night. And they overcame him because of the blood of the Lamb, and because of the word of their testimony; and they loved not their life even unto death.

Mark 8:27–37

And Jesus went forth and his disciples, into the villages of Caesarea Philippi: and on the way he asked his disciples, saying unto them, Who do men say that I am? And they told him, saying, John the Baptist; and others, Elijah; but others, One of the prophets. And he asked them, But who say ye that I am? Peter answereth and saith unto him, Thou art the Christ, the Messiah. And he charged them that they should tell no man of him. And he began to teach them, that the Son of man must suffer many things, and be rejected by the elders, and the chief priests, and the scribes, and be killed, and after three days rise again. And he spake the saying openly. And Peter took him, and began to rebuke him. But he turning about, and seeing his disciples, rebuked Peter, and saith, Get thee behind me, Satan; for thou mindest not the things of God, but the things of men. And he called unto him the multitude with his disciples, and said unto them, If any man would come after me, let him deny himself, and take up his cross, and follow me. For whosoever would save his life shall lose it; and whosoever shall lose his life for my sake and the gospel's shall save it. For what doth it profit a man, to gain the whole world, and forfeit his life? For what should a man give in exchange for his life?

But be not ye called Rabbi: for one is your teacher, and all ye are brethren. And call not man your father on the earth: for one is your Father, even he who is in heaven. Neither be ye called masters: for one is your master, even the Christ. But he that is greatest among you shall be your servant. And whosoever shall exalt himself shall be humbled: and whosoever shall humble himself shall be exalted.

Shall we have a word of prayer:

Beloved Lord, we thank You that You are here present with us, and we have been worshipping You, praising You and thanking You, giving some expression to the adoration of our hearts for You. And, Lord, we now ask that You will fill this time with Your power and anointing. Thank You that You have won for us all an anointing of grace and power through the finished work of our Lord Jesus at Calvary. And You have made that anointing in its fullest extent available to us in the Person of the Holy Spirit. We simply bow before You. We are nothing in ourselves, Lord, but we thank You that You are everything and all we need is in You. Meet us, Lord, and by Your Spirit, confront us, challenge us, meet us. Where there is unreality, bring reality. Where there is sham, bring the essence, the substance. Lord, bring us into a new and deeper experience of Your so-great salvation and of everything that our Lord Jesus so dearly won for us. Into that anointing grace and power we stand now by faith both for the speaking of Your Word, for the translating of Your Word and for the hearing of it. And we shall be careful, Lord, to give You all the praise and all the glory for answering this our prayer. We ask it in the name of our Messiah, the Lord Jesus. Amen.

No Overcoming Apart From Losing the Self-Life

In Revelation 12:11 there are three constituents in overcoming: "And they overcame Satan because of the blood of the Lamb, and because of the word of their testimony; and they loved not their life even unto death" (Revelation 12:11). Now I want to consider the third of those constituents in overcoming: "and they loved not their life even unto death." There can be no overcoming of any sort, on any level, without the losing of our self-life. Our self-life is the biggest single problem in Christian circles. Whether it is in the building of the church, the work of God, or in the individual believer's life, if you and I are not prepared to lose our self-life for His sake and the gospel's, we will get no further than conversion. We will remain converted, believers born of the Spirit of God, but there can be no growth, no progress, no advance, nothing.

The Word of God speaks about the fullness of the Godhead being in the Lord Jesus in bodily form, and in Him we are made complete. This remains a kind of motto without any meaning, without any reality, without any experience for many Christians. It is something we believe in, but it is like a fairytale. The "unsearchable riches of Christ" of which the apostle Paul speaks remains another motto, another sentence of Scripture, without any real meaning. We have never discovered the riches. We can never experience the riches when we have an intact self-life—unbroken, uncrucified, and unyielding to the Lordship of Jesus.

God's Riches in the Messiah Jesus

So much is ours. God has not given us things; He has given us His Son. And in His Son He has given us everything—unsearchable riches, every blessing in heavenly places—not just a few but innumerable blessings in Him (see Ephesians 1:3), and every need of ours supplied according to God's riches in the Messiah Jesus. There is a fathomless fullness, but it all remains in the category of doctrine unless you and I are prepared to lay down our self-life which is our great problem.

The Self-Life Lies at the Bottom of All Problems

There is not a single person—regardless of our ethnic grouping—who does not have a self-life. In this body of ours is an uncrucified, unyielding, unbroken self-life. There may be some who have already yielded to the Lord; they have allowed the Holy Spirit to do His work in them and have moved beyond that stage. But many of us have a self-life, and it is so powerful that it will not allow Jesus to be Lord. He can be our Savior; we are willing for Him to save us, willing for Him to bring us to a new birth, willing for Him to bring us into the kingdom of God, but beyond that we will go no further. We must be in control of our own destiny, of the way we do things, and of our own lives. It is this "unlost", unbroken self-life which is the problem.

There is no problem with sin; it can be dealt with. We can confess our sin and He is faithful and just to forgive us our sins and to cleanse us from all unrighteousness (see 1 John 1:9). But it is the self-life that lies at the root of sin: "I first, I last, and I in between." My life begins with *I*, and ends with *I*; and everything in it is an expression of me. That is the self-life.

It is no good saying nice things because your self-life will destroy you. It will see to it that you do not grow in the Lord or you never enter into all that He died for you to experience. It will make sure that your life is poverty stricken and entangled with a besetting sin, and a thousand and one other things. So simple is this matter: "They overcame him because of the blood of the lamb"—the finished work of the Lord Jesus. "They overcame him (Satan) because of the word of their testimony, and they loved not their life even unto death." This is not just the question of martyrdom; it may include that, but it is more than that. If you are not prepared to lose your self-life, to lay it down, you will never be a martyr; for given a chance you will squirm out of it. You will somehow or other save and preserve your life. This is the challenge—not of the apostle Paul merely nor of the other apostles—of the Lord Jesus Himself.

Death and Resurrection

Mark's gospel recorded Jesus asking His disciples: "Who do men say that I am?" And they said, "This one and that one and the other one." "But who do you say that I am?" And Peter said, "You are the Messiah, the Son of the living God." For the first time, and from that point on, Jesus began to speak about His crucifixion, death, burial and resurrection. He had not spoken about it before, and it therefore came as a great shock to the twelve disciples.

It is interesting that the Lord Jesus never spoke about His death without coupling it with His resurrection. Death in itself was not the end; it was resurrection. And that is exactly the same with us. You might think that I am like a Jeremiah who keeps on about this self-life being broken and yielded and crucified. And you might say, "Lance, can we not have something a bit more cheerful than this kind of message? It is very heavy and dark and gives us an image of holiness— such as wearing black, looking dark and miserable, and being afflicted all the time—therefore, we must be like that if we are going to be real Christians." No, no, that is not what we are talking about. Every time the Word of God speaks about being crucified with Christ, it links it with eternal *life* or with the fullness or life.

Death is Swallowed Up with the Fullness of Life

This is the apostle Paul's testimony: I *have been crucified with Christ ...nevertheless, I live*—(Oh! He is back again; he just said he was crucified.) *And the life which I now live, I live by the faith of the Son of God who loved me and gave Himself for me* (see Galatians 2:20). If you count you will find one crucifixion and "live", "life", "live", "live";—*Christ liveth in me*. It is all there. God does not require you to lay down your self-life to be a miserable morbid believer that goes round in circles all the time thinking only of your broken self. Not at all! The Lord's whole purpose is that we should be filled with resurrection power and life and the fruit that comes from resurrection life. That is the purpose of the Lord. He wants to swallow up death with the fullness of life. That is why the Lord Jesus challenges us in this way.

Now we know that Peter was never afraid. Of course, it is interesting that he only acted as spokesman for all the rest. It says once or twice in the synoptic gospels: "And they all said the same." But it was Peter who always put his foot in it, being the first to speak out, to be straight forward, and to say exactly what he thought. He took Jesus aside, and I imagine he took Him by the arm, stopped him from walking, and said: "You cannot do this! It is impossible for the Messiah to be crucified! That is not what we are looking for; You cannot do it!" And Jesus looked him straight in the eye and said, "Get thee behind Me, Satan, for you do not mind the things of God but the things of this world."

If you came to me with a problem and you were trying to get out of the thing, and looking straight in your eyes I said: "Get behind me, Satan!" you would go straight to the brothers and say, "Never ask that brother to come back and speak again. Do you know what he said to me? He looked straight in my eyes and said, 'Get behind me, Satan.' I have never been called Satan in my life. I am a child of God, I belong to the Lord, I am born again. I have never had anyone call me Satan. If he had only said, 'Satan is troubling your mind,' I could have accepted it. If he had said, 'You are thinking negative thoughts,' I would have accepted it, but to look into my eyes and say: 'Get behind me Satan!'—it is too much! How could he do such a thing? I have a reputation, I have rights. It is not right for someone to go round calling me Satan. I do not think I am like Satan."

Deny Self and Take Up the Cross

So important was this matter that Jesus called the whole multitude together with the disciples. No longer was it just the twelve disciples; no longer was it just within the circle of those that were close to Him, but He brought the whole multitude together and then said: "If any man would come after Me, let him deny himself, take up his cross, and follow Me. For whosoever would save his life shall lose it; and whosoever shall lose his life for My sake and the gospel's, the same shall save it" (see Mark 8:34b–35).

The Lord has issued a challenge here. It is all to do with the gospel. It is not deeper teaching, it is not something you younger ones can put off for a few years in order to enjoy yourselves down here—especially your self-life while you are young and happy. You believe that there will come a time when you will have to start living properly, and when that happens, then is the time to start thinking about giving up your self-life. That is not what it says here. Jesus was saying that this is something to do with the gospel; this is something to do with the death, burial and resurrection of the Lord Jesus. It is as if the Lord Jesus was saying: "By My death, burial and resurrection I have saved you with a tremendous salvation; but you will never know its outworking; you will never know the full power of it, or the fullness of it if you hold on to your self-life."

Follow Me

Consider these two words: "Follow Me." In between those two words comes this: "Deny yourself and take up your cross." In other words, what the Lord Jesus was saying to the whole crowd was simply this: "If you want to follow Me, there is no other way than to deny your self-life and take up the cross." It could not be simpler: "If any man follow Me, let him deny himself, take up his cross and follow Me." You can be a convert and, like Lot's wife, become a memorial to something that happened—dead, no growth, no advance, no progress, and no fullness. Following the Lord speaks of progress, it speaks of advance, it speaks of service, it speaks of His work. There can be no following of the Lord without the losing of your self-life.

Listen again, "If any man follow Me ... and follow Me." What is between those two words "follow"? "Deny himself." This word is a very interesting word in the Greek. It means "renounce yourself", "disavow yourself", "disown yourself", "give up all right to yourself".

We live in a world of rights. Everything has "rights." Trees have rights, plants have rights, flowers have rights, animals have rights, birds have rights, fish have rights, women have rights—only men have no rights in this world. There are national rights, political rights, ethnic rights; everything is rights. We are mollycoddled with this word "rights." I have my rights. "I am not going to have any one walk over me or control me or be lord and master over me. I have rights!" But Jesus said there is no way that the fullness of your salvation can become your experience without giving up all rights to yourself. What did He mean? He meant that He has to be Lord of your self. Until you yield the Lordship and mastery to Him, there is a blockage in your spiritual life. You can only advance in knowledge, in teaching, and in those kinds of academic things or mentally appreciated matters. You cannot come to know Him deeply and more fully unless you deny yourself.

Take Up His Cross

Here is another matter: "Take up his cross." What we have done in Christian circles over this is incredible. Some people's rheumatic pains are their cross; other people have migraines, and that is their cross. Other people have a husband, and they say that is their cross. Some have wives they say is their cross. Some have children, and that is their cross. It is incredible to me how we have taken this word of our Lord Jesus and devalued its meaning. The cross is the cross. It is not just an ache here, a pain there or a difficult person or relationship; although these may lead you to the cross. The cross is the cross. Jesus was crucified on that tree. How can we devalue such a thing to be an ache or a pain or a headache or a difficult relationship? It is impossible to do it.

We Lose to Gain

From much historical and archeological research we have discovered that generally speaking, certainly in Jerusalem, the stake of the cross was already in place. The person sentenced to death carried a notice round his neck with his crimes written on it, and he bore on his shoulders the crossbeam as he was led to the place of crucifixion. This is what the apostle Paul said in II Corinthians: "Having the sentence of death within ourselves, that we should not trust in ourselves, but in God who raises the dead" (see 1:9). It is another wonderful picture of death, life, and God who raises the dead. Where there is a death there will be a resurrection. If we are willing to lay down our self-life, we will receive it again under new management. We lose our self-life to save it, and the poison in it has been taken out.

Some people think of the cross as a kind of ecstatic experience. If anyone has had an ecstatic experience of being crucified with Christ, I can tell you straightway it is demonic and has nothing to do with reality. To be crucified with Christ is exactly what it says. We are nailed to the cross. In Him we died; He died as you and me. When that becomes a living experience and reality, it is the gateway to resurrection life and resurrection power. Paul said, "We have received the sentence of death within ourselves that we should not trust in ourselves but in God who raises the dead." We should not trust in ourselves. We have received the sentence of death and are on the way to the place of crucifixion. Once we see this matter and are prepared to yield the mastery and ownership of our self-life to the Lord Jesus, the Holy Spirit will lead us to the place of crucifixion. In practice it can be anything—it can be at work, at home, in the church—but it will happen. When we accept a sentence of death upon our self-life, in that moment the journey begins.

Under New Management

There are two words for "life" in Greek. One is used for spiritual life or eternal life, and the other is used for soul-life or self-life. This word as it is translated in my American Standard Version is to do with the self-life: "If any man follow Me, let him deny himself, take up his cross and follow Me. For whosoever would save his soul-life [self-life], will lose it. And whosoever will lose his self-life for My sake and the gospel's, the same shall find it." You lose it to find it. It is amazing what the Lord can give back to us once it is under His management. However, some things never come back.

When I was a little boy I had an obsession with scissors, and probably this will seem very strange to some of you. Nevertheless, I loved scissors—kitchen scissors, my mother's cosmetic scissors, shears for cutting plants. I was all the time trying to get hold of scissors, and when I did, I would toddle around with them clasped to my bosom as if they were made of gold and were priceless. And my mother would go round saying, "Lalla, give me those scissors!" And I would say, "No!" And she would say: "Give-me-those-scissors!" "No!" And she would pull them out of my hands! I thought to myself: "My mother is an absolute witch that she would take these scissors from me. What is wrong with scissors? They are everywhere in the house." It did not mean that I would never use scissors or shears, but my mother knew very well that it could destroy or injure me at that stage in my life. And that is what happens with the Lord when we lose our self-life.

I remember for years I never went to a movie house or saw a film. I even thought television was a little bit sort of spicy. It is amazing. Why did the Lord say to me so early in my Christian life: "Give me this"? And I gave it to Him, as did my sister also. My mother used to say: "I have a monk and nun as son and daughter. They are so pure." Little did she know, but that is what she thought. Of course, we grew up, and the Lord gave us back certain things. Some things He never gives back, others He does as we grow. However, the great point is this: there is One who loved us so much that He died for us and in dying for us, He wants everything that is good for us—everything that will be a blessing and everything that will be spiritually useful. And when He asks us to give up certain things such as a relationship, a friendship, something in the world or whatever else, it is because He is testing us as to whether He really is Lord.

This challenge of the Lord Jesus is quite extraordinary because He goes on as if it is just the gospel: "What shall a man give in exchange for his soul, for his life? What will it profit a man if he gain the whole world and lose his own soul?" This challenge of the Lord is tremendous. No person can follow the Lord Jesus very far before they find in their path the cross, bloody and inescapable.

If you are not prepared for it you will remain a convert and never become a disciple.

Peter Discovers the Poison of the Serpent

Peter is the great illustration of this because he had such a massive self-life. He was not afraid of it nor did he hide it. He was never one of these timid, modest people. He was a rugged fisherman and he said exactly what he thought. However, his Christianity was self-manufactured. He had walked with the Lord for three years, and he thought that he was the chief disciple and that his position was quite clear. He was the one who put into words what the others thought. It was a self-manufactured Christianity. When Jesus looked into his eyes and said, "Get thee behind me, Satan," actually He was saying the truth. In your self-life and in my self-life is the poison of hell, the poison of Satan, the poison of the serpent. It is here in our self-life. That is the result of the fall. That poison in you and me will destroy fellowship with other believers; it will cause division and faction; it will make it difficult for us to be built together with other believers. That kind of poison within my self-life destroys marriages, wrecks families, and brings all kinds of problems into being.

Moses Met the Lord in the Burning Bush

Do you remember when Moses met the Lord in the burning bush that burned with fire? These dried-up thorn bushes were something Moses had seen many times being suddenly and spontaneously ignited by the sun.

When I did guard duty in the RAF[1] we saw it again and again, and I would say to the Bedouin who was with me, "What is that flash of fire?" And he would reply, "Just a thorn bush." Moses saw this bush burning and said to himself: "Here is a thorn bush that has gone up in fire." A few minutes later he looked back and noticed it was still burning. A half an hour later he looked and saw that the bush was still burning. One hour later he decided to go and see this thing. What kind of thorn bush could this be that it burned for an hour? When he came near to the thorn bush, God spoke from the ground up to Moses and said, "Take your shoes off your feet, the ground whereon you stand is holy" (see Exodus 3:5). Then the Lord revealed His great name: I AM that I AM, and told him that he had to go to Pharaoh. And Moses said, "I stutter," which, of course, was nonsense. That is self-life. He said, "I, I, I ... stutter." And the Lord said to him with great humor, "Then take Aaron; he will do the speaking." But Aaron never did the speaking; Moses did it all. However, the Lord was not going to stand and argue.

Then Moses said, "Give me a sign."

And the Lord said, "What is that in your hand?"

And Moses said, "That is my rod."

"What do you do with that rod?"

"Well, with it, I prod the sheep, goats and camels; also I use it sometimes to ward off wild animals that attack us in the night, and it is really a symbol of authority."

Then the Lord said, "Throw it on the ground." And in that moment it became a sand viper, as we know from the Hebrew. It is the most venomous snake in the Sinai Desert. And when Moses

1 Royal Air Force

saw it, he fled. He had been 40 years shepherding sheep, goats, camels and donkeys; he knew very well what a sand viper was. It was a terrible shock to him. "You mean that rod I had beside me when I go to sleep has got a sand viper inside of it? How is that possible?" And then the Lord said, "Moses! Come back! Take up that sand viper by the tail." And I can imagine Moses looking at the Lord and saying, "Did I hear You rightly? I am getting old at 80." "Take him up by the tail!" "Lord?" We all know you never take a sand viper up by the tail. Nevertheless, Moses took him up by the tail and it became a rod. That rod was the rod which the Lord used, that divided the Red Sea, that brought water out of the rock, that did miracle after miracle before Pharaoh and all through the 40 years of Moses' life before he went to be with the Lord.

What is the picture? It is very simple. That rod was the symbol of his divine service, the symbol of his authority, of his very being and the person he was. There was a venom and poison of a serpent in it and he did not know it.

Dear child of God, in your self-life—un-yielded, unbroken, un-crucified—there is the serpent; it is the poison of Satan. That poison will destroy your fellowship, it will destroy your ministry, it will destroy your service, it will destroy your marriage, it will destroy your home, unless you let it go. It was faith that enabled Moses to pick up the serpent by the tail which then again became the rod.

Peter's Self-Manufactured Christianity

Let's come back to Peter for a moment. The Lord Jesus said, "Get behind me, Satan." He knew exactly what He was saying. There was within the self-manufactured Christian life of Peter the poison of the serpent. He even tried to stop Jesus from going to the cross. Yes, he wanted the best for Jesus. That is why in one of the other gospels this same event is recorded with this extra statement: "You are a stumbling block to Me. Get thee behind me, Satan." Do you think that you could be a stumbling block to the Lord? Do you think that in some way or other you could be the destroyer of the very thing that you desire and that He desires for you?

I knew a certain lady on this North American Continent, and she never talked about anything else other than the church. But we all knew she was the destroyer of any possibility of the church being built in the place where she lived. She was taken up with it completely; she could give you a whole message on it; but undefeated the poison was there.

Peter's Restoration

Jesus said: "Simon, Simon, Satan has obtained you by request that he might sift you as wheat." It was that incredible time when Jesus was betrayed and they all fled. The Lord had said to Peter: "Before the cock crows you will have denied me three times." And Peter, with all his self-manufactured Christianity, had denied the Lord three times with oaths before a little slip of a serving girl, a waitress. In that moment the Holy Spirit swept away everything on the surface in Peter's life. Like a nuclear explosion, it blasted everything to nothing. And Peter wept. And this is the amazing thing; Jesus never said a word but just looked at Peter. And in that moment when Peter's eyes and the eyes of Jesus met, Peter was restored. This time it was another kind of life. He had lost his self-life and found it. Now Peter could truly become the chief of the apostles.

It was Peter who ushered in the coming of the Holy Spirit with those wonderful words that we have in Acts 2. It was Peter who ushered the Samaritans into the kingdom of God. It was Peter who ushered in the Gentiles in that drawing room in Caesarea which was filled with Gentile officers and their men. It cost Peter everything, and Satan was the agent. I remember C.T. Studd once said, (and he got into a lot of trouble over it from Christians): "Satan is God's greatest servant, for everything he ever does God uses it to glory." Satan sifted him—Satan got the chaff and God got the wheat.

Giving Up the Keys of Our Life to the Lord

The fact of the matter is this: you and I have a self-life. What are you going to do about it? Young people, what are you going to do about this self-life of yours? It will be your ruination if you do not do something. Somewhere or other you have got to face up to this whole question. You cannot avoid it, you cannot pretend it is not there or ignore it as if somehow or other by so doing you will get out of this problem; you cannot get out of it. You cannot follow the Lord Jesus unless you disavow and disown your self-life and take up His cross.

We want reality, do we not? We want above everything else to be in a real genuine experience of the Lord Jesus. You can never be too young. I was twelve and a half when I gave myself to the Lord. I was devoted to the Lord, but it was two or three years later that I said to the Lord: "Here are the keys to my life; take them, and do with me what You will." You can never start too early. If you will only start right now, God will take in hand your education, training, and discipline until you become a disciple. And of course we never end being disciples. We are always learning more and experiencing more of the Lord.

If any man follow Me, let him deny himself, give up all right to Himself, take up his cross and follow Me; for whosoever shall lose his self-life for My sake and the gospel's, the same shall find it. And they overcame Satan because they loved not their lives even unto death. What are you going to do about this matter? May God reach every heart.

Shall we pray:

Lord, reach every heart, not only the old but the young. Help us, Lord. We want You to have dealings with us. Help us to be real, to be honest, and to be truthful in this matter. None of us want to sacrifice our self-life. None of us want someone else to be master of our lives, but there is no other way. Nevertheless, Lord, You have our best interests at heart—our joy, our fulfillment, the fullness of life and power—You have glory in mind. Lord, challenge us and meet us. We ask it in the name of our Lord Jesus. Amen.

5.
Overcoming Through Being a Living Sacrifice

Revelation 12:10–11

And I heard a great voice in heaven, saying, Now is come the salvation, and the power, and the kingdom of our God, and the authority of his Messiah: for the accuser of our brethren is cast down, who accuseth them before our God day and night. And they overcame him because of the blood of the Lamb, and because of the word of their testimony; and they loved not their life even unto death.

Romans 12:1–21

I beseech you therefore, brethren, by the mercies of God, to present your bodies a living sacrifice, holy, acceptable to God, which is your spiritual service. And be not fashioned according to this world: but be ye transformed by the renewing of your mind, that ye may prove what is the good and acceptable and perfect will of God.

For I say, through the grace that was given me, to every man

---

that is among you, not to think of himself more highly than he ought to think; but so to think as to think soberly, according as God hath dealt to each man a measure of faith. For even as we have many members in one body, and all the members have not the same office: so we, who are many, are one body in Christ, and severally members one of another. And having gifts differing according to the grace that was given to us, whether prophecy, let us prophesy according to the proportion of our faith; or ministry, let us give ourselves to our ministry; or he that teacheth, to his teaching; or he that exhorteth, to his exhorting: he that giveth, let him do it with liberality; he that ruleth, with diligence; he that showeth mercy, with cheerfulness.

Let love be without hypocrisy. Abhor that which is evil; cleave to that which is good. In love of the brethren be tenderly affectioned one to another; in honor preferring one another; in diligence not slothful; fervent in spirit; serving the Lord; rejoicing in hope; patient in tribulation; continuing stedfastly in prayer; communicating to the necessities of the saints; given to hospitality. Bless them that persecute you; bless, and curse not. Rejoice with them that rejoice; weep with them that weep. Be of the same mind one toward another. Set not your mind on high things, but condescend to things that are lowly. Be not wise in your own conceits. Render to no man evil for evil. Take thought for things honorable in the sight of all men. If it be possible, as much as in you lieth, be at peace with all men. Avenge not yourselves, beloved, but give place unto the wrath of God: for it is written, Vengeance belongeth unto me; I will recompense, saith the Lord. But if thine enemy hunger, feed him; if he thirst, give him to drink: for in so doing thou shalt heap coals of fire upon his head. Be not overcome of evil, but overcome evil with good.

Shall we pray:

Beloved Lord, we are so thankful we are here in Your presence. We sense You are here. We worship You, dear Lord. We are not asking you to join us; we are coming to be with You. We want You to speak to us and reveal something more of Your heart and mind to us. And Lord, You have promised us that You are watching over Your Word to perform it. Now that is exactly what we need. We need You to watch over this Word of Yours to perform it. Make it reality in every one of our lives. To that end, Lord, we want to tell You that without the anointing we can only speak words and outline truths. We need that anointing grace and power that You have provided for us through the finished work of our Lord Jesus. And into that anointing we stand by faith, Lord, that You will give a full portion of it, not only for the speaking of Your Word, but for the translating of it and for the hearing of it. Lord, bring everything under that anointing. Anoint the tent of meeting, as it were. Let everything come under that anointing grace and power and fullness that You have won for us and made a living reality in the Person of the Holy Spirit. And we shall be careful to give You all the praise and worship of our hearts for answering this prayer of ours. We ask it in the name of our Messiah, the Lord Jesus. Amen.

What is overcoming? We know that there have been so many who through this whole church age, century after century, have laid down their lives in faithfulness to the Lord Jesus; they overcame. But overcoming is not just martyrdom because the deepest instinct in our being is to preserve ourselves. And if we were faced with death or denial of the Lord, or compromise, many of us would choose compromise or even denial.

I remember the story of Wang Míng-Dao, who, after that incredibly powerful ministry in Beijing, was taken into custody, brainwashed, and then sent to prison—but he compromised. As a result of this he could neither rest nor sleep until he called the authorities and took back his confession and the compromise he had made. They did not kill him; but the wonderful thing is that like all of us, when it came to the final analysis he was tempted, and he gave in to it; however, he discovered that he could not live at peace, and he took back his denial of the Lord. He firmly spoke of his trust and faith in the Lord Jesus, even though it could have meant his death.

If you and I have not laid down our self-life, this instinct to preserve ourselves is so strong it will undo us. That is why in the final analysis those words of the Lord Jesus are so important: *If any man follow me, let him give up all right to himself, take up his cross and follow me. For whosoever would save his life, his soul-life, his self-life, shall lose it. And whosoever shall lose his soul-life, his self-life, for my sake and the gospel's shall find it* (see Mark 8:34–35). We overcome not only through the blood of the Lamb, not only through the word of our testimony, but through not loving our lives even to death. There is no other way to overcome.

What Is an Overcomer?

What is overcoming? We often get this idea that overcomers are a superior or elitist kind of group, a special kind of Christian that knows no fear and is a superman. It is not true. Every child of God is meant to be an overcomer. The Lord has so designed our salvation that when we experience it fully, we become overcomers. We can do no other. Consider this question: If Jesus is really in you, can you be anything else than an overcomer? Let me ask it again: If the Lord Jesus is alive in you, dwelling by the Holy Spirit in your body and in your spirit, can you be anything else than an overcomer? The answer has to be: "No, I can be nothing else. If He really lives in me, if He is really here in power, if He is here as Lord, if my will has been surrendered to Him, if He has the right to do with me anything He wants to do, I can be nothing else than an overcomer. Whatever affliction comes to me, whatever circumstances are mine, whatever difficult relationships I come into, I can be no other than an overcomer.

I once asked brother Sparks many years ago what an overcomer was. We were in his home in Scotland on a cool evening, and there was a fire burning. I remember him looking into it for a while, and knowing Mr. Sparks and how he could sit for half an hour or an hour without saying a word while you became more and more uncomfortable, I waited. After a few long moments of looking into the fire he then said: "An overcomer is someone who is in the full will of God at the end of their life."

I have sometimes heard people use the term "gaining the victory" when referring to overcoming. I do not really like it. After I was saved I was brought up on "victory, victory, victory" all the time, but nobody had the victory. All those wonderful people would sing songs such as "my chains fell off," then I found out afterwards the chains were certainly still on them. They would also sing that the Lord was the answer or "the double cure" of sin. We would sing that hymn with great gusto. And the pastor always spoke about victory. Years later I asked him if he had really experienced that victory or did he just preach about it. And he said, "I preached it in faith, but I did not have it." So that meant not only did the whole congregation live defeated lives but so did the pastor. I was always a little afraid of "gaining the victory." Of course, it is that, and theologically that is right. I am not arguing with those who teach this, but it just disturbs me. I like the term "overcoming" because it means we are coming over. In other words, we are actually coming over the obstacles. When there is some difficulty, we come over it. Where there is a mountain, we traverse over it or remove it by faith. To me overcoming is something so simple.

In the sea we have something called buoys to which you tie boats. When there is a storm the waves go over it and the buoy goes under until you cannot see it, and then suddenly it comes up with the water pouring off it. There is something in the buoy you cannot defeat. It always comes up because it is its nature. It is the same with overcoming. If the Lord Jesus is in you, you can do no other. Even if you go down under a problem, in the end you will come up because He is in you.

In the World You Shall Have Tribulation

The Lord Jesus said in John's gospel: *In Me ye shall have peace* (see 16:33). Do you not have peace in the Lord? I do. In the worst circumstances I find in Him—not in the circumstances—that I have peace. *In the world you shall have tribulation.* I find that also. Now is that not an amazing thing? And then He continued.

When I first came to the Lord, I only had a little booklet of John's gospel. Nobody bothered to give me a Bible or even inquire if I had a Bible, but I read that little gospel of John through and through and through so many times until it fell to pieces. I remember reading this portion and thinking how unfair of the Lord it was: *In Me you shall have peace, in the world you shall have tribulation but be of good cheer I have overcome the world.* I thought that was a terrible thing for Him to say "but be of good cheer *I have overcome* the world." And I thought to myself in my arrogant way, "Well, isn't the Lord saying something! He is almost laughing at us—'but be of good cheer *I have overcome.*'" I was young, about thirteen. Then I discovered what it really means. Why did He not say, "But be of good cheer, you shall be overcomers"? He never said that; He said, *But be of good cheer, I have overcome the world.* In other words, when He is dwelling in you, when He is untrammeled by your will, your stubbornness, your obstinacy, your plans for your life, when you have let go of that self-life, when He is Lord, He will overcome in you. There is no other way. That is overcoming. So we come back to this question of loving not our lives even to the death. If we love our lives, we hinder and frustrate the Lord's plan and strategy to be the overcomer in us. We have a civil war going on inside our own being.

A Living Sacrifice

The passage in Romans 12 is one of the most extraordinary chapters in Romans. Many of you know that it is generally accepted by Bible teachers and theologians that the Roman letter is the greatest exposition of the gospel in the 66 books of the Bible. It is the clearest exposition of the gospel and the greatest interpretation of the gospel that we have in the Bible. The apostle Paul takes the first eight chapters to explain that gospel, and then he takes three more chapters to talk about the Jewish question: "And if God can forsake the Jewish people, can he not also forsake the church?" Then he sums up the whole thing in chapter 12 by saying: "I beseech you, I urge you, by the mercies of God (not even mercy, but *mercies* of God that I have spoken of in those eight chapters and then chapters nine to eleven), to present your bodies a living sacrifice holy, acceptable to God which is your spiritual service."

Set Apart for the Lord

Those of you who know your Bibles will know very well that a living sacrifice could not be maimed or lame or half-blind or spotted with some kind of disease. The sacrifice for the offerings had to be without blemish, without wrinkle, without spot or without any such thing. It had to be a perfect representative of the sheep, the goats, the bullocks or the birds. So what is the apostle saying? *I beseech you therefore, brethren, by the mercies of God to present your bodies a living sacrifice, wholly and acceptable, set apart.* The intrinsic meaning of holiness is to be set apart to God, well pleasing to God, acceptable to Him. Can anyone claim to be a candidate for a living sacrifice if that is the case? The best of us here today have spots or wrinkles or something that renders us unacceptable and unholy. But the gospel he preached is all about Jesus dying in our place, and we, through His death on the cross, through His bearing the punishment of our sins, are declared righteous in the sight of God and clothed with the righteousness of the Lord Jesus.

Clothed in the Righteousness of Christ

In the II Corinthian letter the apostle Paul puts it this way: *Him who knew no sin he made to be sin on our behalf ; that we might become the righteousness of God in Him* (5:21). That means we are justified. He became our sin and we have become the righteousness of God in Him. This gospel is incredible! And in those three chapters from nine to eleven he speaks about the grace of God on vessels of mercy afore prepared for glory. This gospel that he has preached to us in this incredible letter which he has written to explain and interpret it, leads up to this: "Now then you are living sacrifices. You have neither spot nor wrinkle in the sight of God; you are not maimed, nor lame; there is nothing wrong about you. You are clothed in the righteousness of Christ." You might say, "Surely you are not calling us to be living sacrifices if we are clothed in the righteousness of Christ. We are kings! We are royal priests. Surely we are called into royal service by God. We are sort of *above*." "No," he says, "you are to be living sacrifices—not dead sacrifices—holy, acceptable to God which is your spiritual service." This is the end of the gospel, the goal of the gospel. Again you might say, "We should be children of God and filled with glory." Absolutely! "We should be changed into the likeness of the Lord Jesus." Absolutely! You can also add a few more things as well, but the aim of the gospel is that you should be a living sacrifice. And so we come back to the verse: "They overcame Satan because they loved not their life even unto death" (Revelation 12:11).

A Living Sacrifice is to be Burned on the Altar

What is a living sacrifice for? To be burned up on the altar. For some people that does not sound like the gospel. "Oh no," they say, "the gospel is that once you are converted and brought to the Lord, washed in His blood, you will be carried by angels on a bed of roses the whole way into glory. That is the gospel. There is no tribulation, no affliction, no fellowship of His sufferings, no antagonism from the Devil because he has been beaten already and gone off to his own place." No, there is something tremendous here—a living sacrifice. This is the aim of the gospel. You might reply: "Do you mean that glory is not the aim of the gospel?" Of course, glory is the aim of the gospel—the glory of God. "Are you saying that we are not to be transformed into the likeness of the Lord Jesus?" No, I am not; that is the purpose of the Lord. What I am saying is this: Unless you and I become living sacrifices there is no progress, no advance, and no growth. Here we are back to the same matter as before. If you love your life over everything else and hold on to it, cling to it, and seek to preserve it, there is no possibility of your moving forward. You are stuck like so many.

John the apostle wrote later in one of his letters about the faith that has been given to us. He said: *For whatsoever is begotten of God overcometh the world: and this is the victory that hath overcome the world, even our faith* (1 John 5:4). This faith is all to do with *"the Son of God"* with believing *"in Him"* and beholding *"Him"*. This is how we overcome. We overcome the world as we behold the Lord Jesus.

The Consequences of Being a Living Sacrifice

The consequences of this are incredible as we have seen in this chapter. The Lord Jesus has borne our sin away and clothed us in His righteousness. Of course this does not mean there is no sin to be confessed; *If we say we have no sin we lie* (see 1 John 1:8), but it does mean that we are clothed with His righteousness, and we can be that living sacrifice.

Spiritual Service

The first consequence is spiritual service. *I [urge you], I beseech you therefore, brethren, by the mercies of God, to present your bodies a living sacrifice, which is your spiritual service* (see Romans 12:1). Now the Greek here is very interesting. If we look at all the different versions we will find almost as many translations. Years ago I remember puzzling over this because "reasonable service" did not seem to me to be spiritual service. At that time we had in the fellowship a Cambridge don in Greek, so I went to him and asked him about it, and he said he would look it up. I had said to him, "I wonder whether I could translate it *spiritually intelligent service*. When he returned a day later he said,

"It is very interesting, but that is the best way to translate it. It is very difficult to get the real meaning across; nevertheless, we have to add one other word: your *spiritually intelligent "worship" and service*. The first consequence of being a living sacrifice is that it is your spiritually intelligent worship and service.

Now there is nothing wrong about having emotion in worship. After all, Mary herself said: *My soul doth magnify the Lord, and my spirit hath rejoiced in God my Saviour* (Luke 1:46-47). What began in her spirit got into her soul. Can there be worship without some emotion, without some feeling? I know some people believe we should not have musical instruments and only use the human voice. I have never understood that. But I remember once talking with a dear brother in one of the strangest assemblies I have ever known in Scotland. They had this thing about music, and it came as a result of them seeing in the Word that everything had to be baptized because that is the new creation. When it has gone through baptism, it is the new creation. So they baptized the organ—not by sprinkling but by immersion. Of course, it never played again, and then they put down the piano. It is incredible sometimes what we get into as the Lord's children.

What is real worship? Real worship is not just being touched by emotion for the moment which will be transient and passing, but this kind of worship leads you in a cold-blooded way to lose your self-life. To become a living sacrifice is your spiritually intelligent worship. It means you have thought it through and with your will surrendered to His will, you have offered yourself as a living sacrifice.

The same is true with your service. We can all be touched. I have met in my lifetime many servants of the Lord who went to different parts of the world to serve Him, and they have told me that they should not have been there. They were caught up in the emotion and excitement of a big missionary meeting and they offered themselves and went. Of course, there are those who have gone by the calling of God. Thank God for them and what they have brought to the nations of the world. But there are those who have made a mistake and were just caught up in the emotion of a moment. However, this kind of service is when you have in a cold-blooded way sat down and said, "Lord, here am I, send me." Such worship rejoices the heart of God as no other worship can. It is reality; it is the heart of the matter.

Fashioned According to This world

This is the second consequence we find in Romans 12: *Be not fashioned according to this world* (12:2a)." That is a good word. Can you tell me of any child of God that is not molded (which is the Greek word), by the fashion of this world? All of us to some extent or another, unless we are really weird, are molded by the fashion of this world—its philosophy, its rationale, the way it does things, the way it thinks, its strategy, its aims, its goals, right down to small things. We cannot help it.

Be not fashioned according to this world. If your self-life is still intact, by your will you will be fashioned according to this world. It is only when you surrender your will to the will of God that for the first time the mold is broken. You are free from being a slave to the philosophy of this world, to the thinking of this world or to the ways of this world. How important this is! No wonder the apostle Paul by the Spirit of God says: *I urge you therefore, by the mercies of God to present your body a living sacrifice. And be ye not—note that he links it—fashioned, molded according to this world.*

Be Transformed by the Renewing of Your Mind

Here is the third thing: *But be ye transformed by the renewing of your mind* (12:2b). The mind is the most important thing. If your mind is not renewed by the Holy Spirit, you will be a slave to the fashion and philosophy of this world. It is only when the Lord can get hold of your mind and renew it that He can transform you. He links transformation with the renewing of your mind. Once your mind is being renewed, you are in the process of being transformed, and you will become like the Lord Jesus. There will be a Christ-likeness in you. What amazing consequences there are in this whole thing!

The Good and Acceptable and Perfect Will of God

And this is the fourth consequence: *That ye may prove what is the good and acceptable and perfect will of God* (12:2c). Now let us be honest with one another and forget all the sham. Does anyone find God's will good, acceptable and perfect? I have lived long enough to know that young people are terribly afraid of the will of God. They think: "If God has His way with me, I will be a monk or a nun. I shall live my whole life alone. If I let the Lord have His way with me I may end up in Timbuktu or Mongolia or somewhere else in the world. And I do not want it." How in the world can a child of God prove what is the good, acceptable and perfect will of God unless they are a living sacrifice, unless that transaction has taken place in their life in which they have surrendered to the Lordship of Jesus and He is Lord in their life? Then for the first time they are able to prove what is the good, acceptable and perfect will of God.

I have not found in my life thus far a single time that the Lord has led me into the doing of His will which has not been good, acceptable and perfect. To begin with I did not think it; I was afraid of it. But once I was ready to obey the Lord, I found that it was good, acceptable and perfect. The problem once again is our self-life that causes all the fuss. "Oh no, the will of God for me could not possibly be good, acceptable and perfect. He wants to put me in a strait jacket. He wants to put me into a little prison or a factory and make me work the whole time for Him. He will exploit me." I have never found any of this to be true. I have found exactly the opposite—that when we are ready to be a living sacrifice, we will prove that the will of God is good, acceptable and perfect. Perfect! Think of it.

Think of Ourselves Soberly

The fifth thing that is the result of being a living sacrifice is to think of yourselves moderately, soberly, with good judgment and modestly. He puts it is this way: *I say, through the grace that was given me, to every man that is among you, not to think of himself more highly than he ought to think; but so to think as to think soberly, according as God hath dealt to each man a measure of faith* (12:3). I think the church scene is beset with people who have very high opinions of themselves, much higher than they ought to have. They think they have this office, this status, this gift, that gift. What a work the Holy Spirit does in us when for the first time we can think of ourselves soberly instead of being drunk with the ideas of who we are or of what we are. We are to think soberly of ourselves. You may not agree with me, but let me tell you a few things. I have seen so many things in my little life. I remember a lady who used to always apprehend us after a church meeting and talk to us. She was from Ireland and she would say, "You know that you can trust me with a confidence: I can keep them." We all knew very well that if you said something to her in confidence and asked her not to tell anyone, the whole town would know within an hour. She had no idea of herself. She thought she was able to keep confidences.

I remember another brother who was a big noise in the Full Gospel Business Men, and he wrote to me on one occasion about another brother who was also a leader, and he said, "You know, dear brother, this man is this, this, this, this and this." It was quite an accusation. And he ended the letter by saying, "Pray for me; you know that I am the humblest man on the face of this earth." Of course, every one of us who knew that dear brother—and he was a good brother— knew very well the one thing he was not, was the humblest man on the face of the earth. He was quite the opposite. He was an incredibly proud man, but he did not know himself.

There are people who believe that they have the gift of speaking and it is dreadful; they just drone on and on and on and send us all to sleep. And there are other people who think they have other kinds of gifts. I shall never forget one sister who believed she had the gift of singing. It was the most dreadful thing I have ever heard in my life. When she sang a solo she managed to hit every note either above it or below it. It was absolutely awful but nobody could tell her. She believed it was a gift from God or a natural talent which she had and she must use it for the glory of the Lord. Well, there was not any glory of the Lord in it but we could not tell her.

One of the reasons why we have to become a living sacrifice is for the division between our spirit and our soul for the first time. It is only then in our Christian experience that we begin to see ourselves objectively. We begin to see not only what is of the Lord in us but also what is not of the Lord. Many times people have come to me and told me that the Lord has said this and this and this to them, but it has not been the Lord who has said that and that and that to them at all. It has been their own soul masquerading as the Spirit of God, and they do not know it. And whenever I have said to them that I did not believe it was the Spirit of God, they said: "How then shall I ever know what is the Lord?" There has to be division between soul and spirit. This is the same thing here.

You are to think soberly according as God has dealt to each one a measure of faith. What is the measure of faith God has given to you? That measure of faith will take you the whole way to the throne of God. If it is a smaller measure and you are a help in the Lord, thank God for that. We could do with any number of helps in the body of Christ. You begin to see that being a living sacrifice is much more than just a word that the apostle Paul used toward the end of this letter.

A Member in the Body of Christ

But here is yet another thing. The consequence or result of being a living sacrifice is that you find yourself within the body of Christ. *One body in Christ, and severally members one of another* (12:5b). If that self-life has never been dealt with, you will experience nothing but sparks flying the whole time—division, faction, clashes, jealousies, rivalries, a thousand and one things. When you have settled the question that you are a living sacrifice, you discover that you are moving in Christ. In Christ—not one body *of* Christ, it is one body *in* Christ; you discover the body and that you are members one of another. You belong to each other. You are sharing the same Lord Jesus. We do not necessarily share the same ethnic background, the same social status, or the same educational background, but the one thing that we have absolutely in common is the Lord Jesus. He is in me and He is in you, and therefore we are members one of another. Is that not amazing?

I have seen many groups come together over the years to set up the church, to be the house of God, and I have also seen them fall apart. The key to the falling apart is the non-existent living sacrifice. It is only when there are people who are living sacrifices that we discover the body. That is overcoming.

Thus, all these things are overcoming—our spiritually intelligent worship and service, being fashioned not according to this world, being transformed by the renewing of our mind, proving what is the good and acceptable and perfect will of God, thinking soberly of ourselves, being able to see ourselves objectively, being able to see what the Lord is doing and what is just our flesh, discovering the body of the Lord in Christ. You are in Christ, I am in Christ. We have the same Christ. I do not have a tailor-made Christ nor do you have a tailor-made Christ. There is only one Christ—you are in Him and I am in Him. He is in you and He is in me; therefore, we now have a double union. We are in the same Christ, and the same Christ is in us.

Now we discover each other and that we are living stones, being built together into a spiritual house to offer up spiritual sacrifices acceptable to God through Jesus the Messiah.

The Priesthood of All Believers

Then we discover that out of this comes the priesthood of all believers. Does a man have a prophetic gift? Let him prophesy. Does he have the gift of exhortation and encouragement? Let him encourage. Is he a teacher? Let him teach. Suddenly we discover that in this one body there are all kinds of different gifts, different positions, as it were, and different ways in which the Lord contributes to the whole (see 12:6–8). It is wonderful.

Spiritual Character

But what are you going to do about the last verses? They are very interesting, are they not? *Let love be without hypocrisy* (12:9a). What has that got to do with the priesthood of all believers? I would call it spiritual character. So out of being a living sacrifice, spiritual character is formed by the Holy Spirit. And this kind of character here is really something. Have you ever had enemies? Have you ever prayed for them? Have you ever blessed them? Have you ever fed them? Have you ever really looked after them— and they are enemies? That is not so easy. "Bless those that revile you." Not so easy. This is another kind of character; it is not the old self-life that is: "I first, I last, and I everywhere between." This is the Lamb of God; it is another kind of character.

I believe that what we have really said about overcoming is that it is to be a living sacrifice. When a person is a living sacrifice, there are a whole number of results. That child of God becomes an overcomer who is very normal—not elite, not a supremacist, not someone who thinks that they are the cat's whiskers, the dog's ears, or that they are wonderful. It is something so normal. They are an overcomer because the Lord Jesus is able to build the house of God through them, and they are able to function in the house of God, and at the same time a spiritual character is being formed in them.

May the Lord challenge every one of us because it comes down to this: Are you prepared to be a living sacrifice? It is not the same as saying: Do you want to be a Hollywood star, do you want to be some big athletic icon, do you want to be someone popular in the world, known by all? Only the Word of God could speak of such a thing, but to be a living sacrifice is the first major step after you have been saved if you are going to progress and grow in the Lord. If the beauty of the Lord Jesus is going to be seen upon you, you have to be a living sacrifice. There is no substitute and there is no alternative. That is why they overcame him through the blood of the Lamb, through the word of their testimony, and they loved not their lives even unto death. May God help you to make a cold-blooded, spiritually intelligent decision.

Shall we pray.

Lord, help us; we need You. This is not a very popular thing to pray about, being a living sacrifice, but it is all part and parcel of Your service, and it is all to do with the effect of the gospel. Challenge us, Lord, challenge us. For we ask it in the name of the Lord Jesus. Amen.

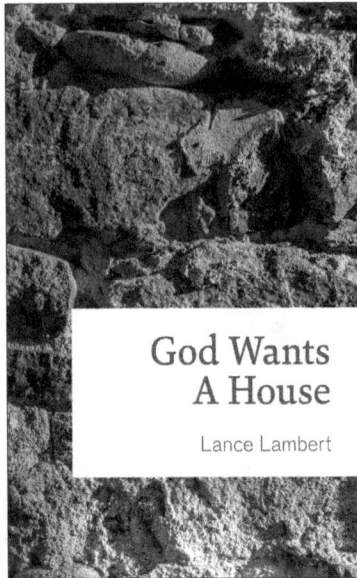

God Wants A House

Where is God at home? Is He at home in Richmond, VA? Is He at home in Washington? Is He at home in Richmond, Surrey? Is He at home in these other places? Where is God at home? There are thousands of living stones, many, many dear believers with real experience of the Lord, but where has the ark come home? Where are the staves being lengthened that God has finally come home? In *God Wants a House* Lance looks into this desire of the Lord, this desire He has to dwell with His people. What would this dwelling look like? Let's seek the Lord, that we can say with David, "One thing have I asked of Jehovah, that will I seek after: that I may dwell in the house of Jehovah all the days of my life, To behold the beauty of Jehovah, And to inquire in his temple."

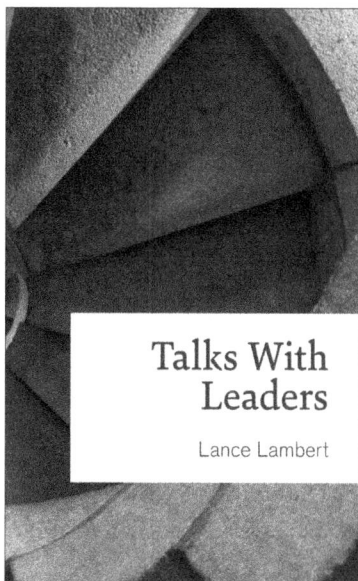

Talks With Leaders

"O Timothy, guard that which is committed unto thee ..."
(1 Timothy 6:20) Has God given you something? Has God
deposited something in you? Is there something of Himself
which He has given to you to contribute to the people of God?
Guard it. Guard that vision which He has given you. Guard that
understanding that He has so mercifully granted to you. Guard
that experience which He has given that it does not evaporate or
drain away or become a cause of pride. Guard that which the Lord
has given to you by the Holy Spirit. In these heart-to-heart talks
with leaders Lance Lambert covers such topics as the character
of God's servants, the way to serve, the importance of anointing,
and hearing God's voice. Let us consider together how to remain
faithful with what has been entrusted to us.

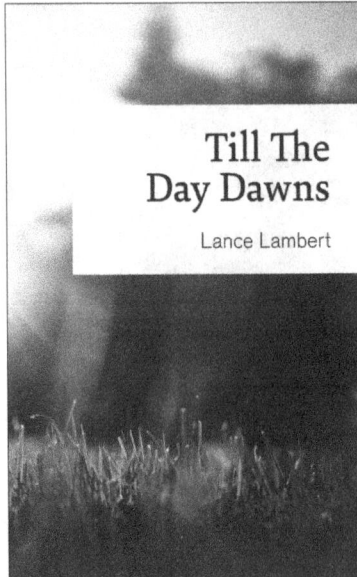

Till the Day Dawns

"And we have the word of prophecy made more sure; whereunto ye do well that ye take heed, as unto a lamp shining in a dark place, until the day dawn, and the day-star arise in your hearts." (II Peter 1:9).

The word of prophecy was not given that we might merely be comforted but that we would be prepared and made ready. Let us look into the Word of God together, searching out the prophecies, that the Day-Star arise in our hearts until the Day dawns.

www.ingramcontent.com/pod-product-compliance
Lightning Source LLC
Chambersburg PA
CBHW060020050426
42448CB00012B/2830